j920   Knotts, Bob.
KNO
          Sports superstars.

$27.95

DATE			

SPORTS SUPERSTARS:

8 OF TODAY'S HOTTEST ATHLETES

Bob Knotts

Sports Illustrated
FOR
KiDS
BOOKS

This Library Edition First Published and Exclusively Distributed by
The Rosen Publishing Group, Inc.
New York

To my wife, Jill; to my parents, Bill and Jeanette; and to my editor, Margaret. Thank you! — B.K.

This library edition first published in 2003 and exclusively distributed by
The Rosen Publishing Group, Inc., New York

Alex Rodriguez chapter written by Alan Schwarz
Marshall Faulk chapter written by Ashley Jude Collie

Book Design: Michelle Innes
Additional editorial material: Nel Yomtov

Photo Credits: Cover (left, right), pp. 7, 35, 49, 63 © Icon Sports Media; cover (center),
p. 93 Chuck Solomon/SI/Icon SMI; all background images © Picturequest; pp. 19, 109
© John Biever/SI/Icon SMI; p. 77 © David Seelig/Icon SMI

First edition

Library of Congress Cataloging-in-Publication Data

Knotts, Bob.
  Sports superstars : 8 of today's hottest athletes / Bob Knotts.
      p. cm.
"Sports illustrated for kids books."
Includes index.
Summary: Profiles eight contemporary athletes whose success in
overcoming obstacles on the path to fame sets an example for others to
follow.
  ISBN 0-8239-3692-9
  1. Athletes—United States—Biography—Juvenile literature. [1.
Athletes.] I. Title.
  GV697.A1 K593 2003
  796'.092'2—dc21

                                        2002002850

>> CONTENTS

>> INTRODUCTION

Every day, something amazing happens in the world of sports. A baseball slugger slams an astounding home run. Or a football quarterback throws a game–winning, last–second touchdown pass. At any time, there's always something and someone to cheer about.

So, how can anyone choose the eight absolute hottest athletes in the world? Easy. We let kids help us figure that out. We looked at the readers' polls conducted by SPORTS ILLUSTRATED FOR KIDS magazine and other research we've done with kids around the country. We found the athletes who aren't just the hottest ones today, but who are going to stay hot. *Sports Superstars: 8 of Today's Hottest Athletes* identifies those athletes and tells their stories.

From the world of pro football, we have running back Marshall Faulk of the St. Louis Rams and quarterback Brett Favre of the Green Bay Packers. Los Angeles Laker Kobe Bryant and San Antonio Spur Tim Duncan are our pro basketball big shots, and Mia Hamm comes from the U.S. Women's Soccer Team. Baseball blasters Ken Griffey, Jr. of the Cincinnati Reds, Alex Rodriguez of the Texas Rangers, and Sammy Sosa of the Chicago Cubs round out the group.

All eight athletes are champions. Many have overcome great obstacles along the path to fame. All of them have become examples to kids who want to be like them. These players are great. They are the Sports Superstars 8!

>> MARSHALL FAULK

Running and receiving, he is the NFL's double-edged sword

On December 26, 1999, the St. Louis Rams were battling the Chicago Bears at the Trans World Dome, in St. Louis, Missouri. After the first period, the score was still 0–0. The Rams' monster offense just couldn't get anything going against the tough Bear defense until . . .

With eight minutes 36 seconds left in the first half, St. Louis had the ball. On second down at the Chicago 48–yard line, the Rams' Marshall Faulk caught a short pass over his shoulder as he darted toward the right sideline. Then he outraced the Bear defenders for a touchdown. The Rams were on their way to a 34–12 victory.

Marshall had 12 receptions for a whopping 204 yards that day. His big day took him over 1,000 receiving yards for the season. Only the best receivers in the NFL gain that many yards in a season.

But Marshall is not a receiver. He's a running back. In fact, he's an All-Pro running back who also rushed for more than 1,000 yards in 1999. In the game against

the Bears, Marshall became only the second running back in NFL history to gain more than 1,000 yards rushing and 1,000 yards receiving in the same season. (Roger Craig of the San Francisco 49ers did it in 1985.)

Marshall's dazzling running and receiving make him one of the most feared offensive weapons in the NFL. When the Rams played the Tennessee Titans in the 2000 Super Bowl, Marshall was held to only 17 yards rushing by the tough Tennessee defense. But the Titans couldn't stop him from catching passes. He ended up with five catches for 90 yards to help the Rams win, 23–16.

"He always amazes me," Ram quarterback Kurt Warner told reporters that season. "He's just a special guy once he gets the ball. There are a lot of times I find myself just sitting back and watching him."

When he's carrying the ball, Marshall is as slippery as an eel. He senses where tacklers are and takes off at the last second, leaving them grasping nothing but air. "It's like Marshall has eyes in the back of his head," Ram running-back coach Wilbert Montgomery told *Sports Illustrated.*

Before the 2000 Super Bowl, reporters asked Marshall why he's so good. He replied, "I can see everything. I'm aware of what's going on. I know a lot about football and what everybody is supposed to be doing."

Each week, Marshall studies the strategies that opposing defenses are likely to use. He is a great listener. He takes pride in remembering lessons taught by his coaches. Marshall has always been fascinated by the X's and O's on the

THE MARSHALL PLAN

The Marshall Faulk Foundation helps kids in poor city neighborhoods like the one in which Marshall grew up. He donated $500,000 to the foundation when he joined the Rams, in 1999. Each time he scores a touchdown, he gives $2,000 to "The Marshall Plan" to help inner-city kids.

coach's chalkboard. That is a good thing because his love of football and his ability to use his mind helped Marshall escape a dangerous childhood that could have brought him down before he ever got started.

MEAN STREETS

Marshall William Faulk was born on February 26, 1973, in New Orleans, Louisiana. He grew up with his five older brothers in the Desire Street housing projects in a neighborhood where violence and drugs ruled the scene. It was like a war zone.

"I had a guy pull a gun on me," said Marshall. "Shooting, guys dying from crack, that was just part of life. It prepared me for other obstacles in my life that I had to overcome."

Marshall's dad, Roosevelt, was rarely at home. He was busy running a restaurant and working for a trucking company. Marshall's mom, Cecile, worked odd jobs while trying to raise her six sons. Marshall's mom and dad divorced when he was only four and his dad died when Marshall was 15.

Marshall's five brothers got into trouble. But they weren't the only ones. Marshall was kicked out of three elementary schools for bad behavior. Guns and drugs took the lives of some of his friends. Life in New Orleans was bad news for the Faulks.

Marshall was lucky that people always seemed to look out for him. In grade school, one of his teachers, Mrs. Porter, helped keep him out of trouble.

"Mrs. Porter reported to my mom on how I was doing in school," says Marshall. "If my grades were bad or if I misbehaved in school, I couldn't play football that week. Mrs. Porter made me miss a lot of games."

At George Washington Carver High School, Marshall's football coach, Wayne Reese, also looked out for Marshall. Coach Reese knew Marshall had the potential to go far in professional sports.

HANGING IN THERE

At one point in high school, Marshall decided to quit football so he could get a job and make some money. Coach Reese told him that a great future lay ahead if he could just hang tough and strive for it. He got Marshall a job as a janitor at the school. Marshall was no stranger to work.

Growing up, he held several jobs such as selling popcorn at New Orleans Saints' home games, working at a shrimp kitchen, and cutting friends' hair. The janitor's job helped Marshall continue to play football and stay in school.

Coach Reese made his players practice before and after school so that they would be too pooped to get into trouble after they left for the day. Somehow, Marshall still found enough time to study football closely and to analyze plays.

Marshall became such a fine all-round player that he played kicker, quarterback, wide receiver, cornerback, and running back for Carver High. During his junior and senior seasons, Marshall rushed for 1,800 yards and scored 32 touchdowns. He also intercepted an impressive 11 passes on defense. Scouts from major colleges wanted him only as a defensive back. Marshall wanted to play running back.

"You get your mind set, and you stick with it," Marshall said. "I'm a firm believer that whatever I want to do, I'm going to do."

So Marshall decided to attend the first college that wanted him as a running back: San Diego State University. Marshall was made to play offense and he knew it. In later years, he said, "Offense is fun for me. There is no chance I would be as good if that was not what I wanted to be doing."

Marshall was listed as the sixth-string running back when he arrived at San Diego State. That meant there were five running backs that would get to play before he did. Marshall changed that in a hurry. He moved up to second-string by impressing his coaches in pre-season practices.

Then, when the team's starting running back was hurt, Marshall got a chance to show what he could do. In only his second game, he set a national college rushing record of 386 yards and scored seven touchdowns. Marshall went on to become the first freshman running back to lead the nation in rushing (1,429 yards).

Marshall won All–America honors and finished in the Top 10 in the voting for the Heisman Trophy in each of his three seasons at San Diego State. During his stay at

THE MARSHALL MINUTE

Birth Date	February 26, 1973
Height	5 feet 10 inches
Weight	211 lbs.
Home	St. Louis, Missouri
College Major	Public Administration
Favorite Foods	Red beans and rice, fried chicken, apple pie with vanilla ice cream
Biggest Sports Thrill	His first TD in the homecoming game as a high school senior
Favorite Cartoon Character	Spider-Man
Favorite Vacation Spot	Hawaii

San Diego State, Marshall set school records for most carries (766) and most rushing yards (4,589). When he decided to enter the 1994 NFL draft after his junior season, the Indianapolis Colts made him the second player chosen.

THE FUTURE ARRIVES

Marshall took the NFL by storm as a rookie. After three quarters of his very first game, against the Houston Oilers, Marshall had rushed for 143 yards and scored three TDs. "This is by no means a fluke," said former Dallas Cowboy star running back Tony Dorsett after witnessing Marshall's performance. "Marshall Faulk is a gift."

In his next game, against the Tampa Bay Buccaneers, he rushed for 104 yards and became the first rookie since 1980 to begin his NFL career with two 100–yard games. The great future Coach Reese predicted for Marshall had arrived.

"You better bring your track shoes and your lunch box to play him," said linebacker Darryl Talley of the Buffalo Bills. "You've got to chase him on first down and on second down, and then on third down he'll catch a pass out of the backfield. When do you ever get a break from this guy?"

After rushing for 1,282 yards, Marshall was chosen as the 1994 Offensive Rookie of the Year. Then he set an NFL record by rushing for 180 yards in the Pro Bowl. He was the only rookie in the game, but he was named the game's MVP.

"I've surprised myself," he said. "No one comes into the NFL and is able to do all the things I've done this fast. It scares me to know I'm being so successful so early. When I learn all the things I need to learn, how good can I be?"

In 1998, his fifth season with the Colts, Marshall led the NFL in total yards and was selected to his third Pro Bowl. But his contract with the Colts was up after the season. The team decided to save money by drafting a young running back and trading Marshall. They sent him to the St. Louis Rams, who had had an awful 4–12 record in 1998 and looked as if they were going absolutely nowhere.

Marshall signed a seven-year $45 million contract with St. Louis, but he was still upset about the trade. Little did Marshall know it at the time, but the Rams' offensive system would be the perfect spot for him to display his versatile physical and thinking skills.

"I was elated to get Marshall," said Rams' vice president of player personnel Charley Armey. "I had studied him carefully when he came out of college . . . He runs with his eyes probably as well as any back in pro football, probably in the history of pro football."

Marshall's concern about the trade to St. Louis were put to rest when he went to a Rams' camp to check out his new teammates. He found a group of talented offensive players, such as wide receivers Isaac Bruce, Torry Holt, Ricky Proehl, and Az-Zahir Hakim.

With Marshall joining the offense, the 1999 Rams became the biggest surprise of the season. Marshall broke the NFL all-purpose yardage record for one season with 1,381 rushing yards and 1,048 receiving yards, for a total of 2,429 yards. He also scored 12 TDs. Marshall was named the 1999 NFL Offensive Player of the Year and earned his fourth trip to the Pro Bowl in six seasons. He also helped the Rams win the Super Bowl.

Ram quarterback Kurt Warner paid his teammate the highest compliment following the Rams' Super Bowl win. "He's like another quarterback on the field. He understands what's going on with the entire system. That sets him apart from other backs . . . The guy is phenomenal."

YOU CAN'T CATCH ME

Phenomenal — and then some. Marshall continued to keep opposing NFL defenders shaking in their boots during the 2000 season.

Marshall played in only 14 games, but he rushed for 1,359 yards and scored a career-high 18 rushing touchdowns. The sure-handed running back added 81 receptions for 830 yards and eight touchdowns. Marshall was named to his fifth Pro Bowl. He was also named the league MVP.

Marshall's best performance came against the New Orleans Saints in the final game of the regular season. He torched the Saints for 220 rushing yards, seven receptions, and three touchdowns. The Rams won the game, 26–21.

The Rams posted a 10–6 record on the season. But they were knocked out of the playoffs in a wild–card game against the Saints, 31–28. Marshall was held to a season–low 24 rushing yards.

In 2001, the Rams were determined to get back to the Super Bowl. Led by quarterback Kurt Warner, St. Louis tore through their opposition, posting a league–leading 14–2 record. The Rams explosive offense scored 503 points — 90 points more than the second–highest scoring team, the Indianapolis Colts.

Marshall had yet another great season in 2001. He rushed for 1,382 yards, caught 83 passes, and scored 21 touchdowns. Marshall became the only player in NFL history with four 2,000–plus yard seasons (rushing and receiving yards combined). He was selected to his sixth Pro Bowl. Marshall was edged out by teammate Kurt Warner for the league's MVP by only four points.

In the playoffs, the Rams crushed the Green Bay Packers, 45–17, in a first–round game. St. Louis then beat the Philadelphia Eagles, 29–24, in the conference championship game. Marshall went wild, rushing for 159 yards — a career–high playoff record — and scoring two touchdowns. Marshall knew it was one of his best games ever. "I left it all out there. I couldn't have written a script better than this," he said.

Once again, the Rams were headed to the Super Bowl. Their opponent would be the New England Patriots. Super Bowl XXXVI, played in New Orleans, Louisiana, would be one to remember. The Patriots shocked the football world with a 20–17 victory over the heavily–favored Rams. And they did it on the most dramatic field goal in Super Bowl history. With no time left on the game clock, Pats' kicker Adam Vinatieri kicked a 48–yard field goal to give New England its first NFL title. It was an amazing finish to one of the finest Super Bowl games ever played.

Marshall didn't have the game he was hoping for in front of his hometown New Orleans fans. The Patriot defense bottled him up, allowing Marshall only 76 yards on 17 carries. The disappointing finish to another great season will surely be an incentive for him in 2002.

A THINKING MAN'S RUNNER

In addition to his speed, quickness, and keen eye, Marshall brings smarts to every game he plays. It's no lie to say that he has an idea of what every player's job is on every play. He understands each player's movements from attending the team meetings and watching videos of each game. "Knowledge relaxes me. Football is all about playing faster. You play faster when you know more," Marshall explains.

But Marshall rarely takes notes and he spends the last minutes before a game not studying, but listening to his favorite song over and over. "Once the game begins, I play to that song in my head. I run to rhythm and that allows my mind to be free," he says.

Marshall is never satisfied with his level of play. After each season, he decides which part of his game needs improving. Then he gets to work. "I want to be better than I was the year before," he says.

For the man who might already be the best player in the NFL, it's going to be scary to see what heights Marshall Faulk will reach.

>> BRETT FAVRE

This quarterback strong-armed his way into the NFL's top ranks

Brett Favre is one of the most dangerous men in the National Football League. The Green Bay Packer quarterback can cut through opposing players faster than a hot knife slices butter. He stands at the line of scrimmage looking over the defense. He stands there, shouting signals, changing plays instantly, if that's what is needed. Once the ball is in his hands, Brett can throw from the pocket or while he's running. Most of the time, Brett's passes are perfect bullets, and often, they go for big touchdowns.

Many of these skills were seen during Super Bowl XXXI, in January 1997. The Packers were playing the New England Patriots. Early in the second quarter, Brett noticed the Patriot defense lining up for man–to–man coverage of Green Bay's three wide receivers. So Brett changed the play on the spot by calling an audible — a coded signal that changes a play just before the ball is snapped. The change allowed Brett to quickly hit his receiver, Antonio Freeman. Touchdown! And what

a touchdown. The scoring play was 81 yards long, and it was the longest touchdown from scrimmage in Super Bowl history. The Packers went on to win the game, 35–21.

Brett is a dangerous man on a football field — and he's not just dangerous to opponents. "He once broke my finger on a pass," recalled Mark Chmura, a Packer tight end. "Sometimes Brett has no idea how hard he throws. Your hands have to be out and ready."

There also have been times when Brett was more dangerous off the gridiron than on it — dangerous to himself. He drank too much alcohol. He became addicted to pain-killing pills that threatened to end his career. . . and maybe his life. Alcohol and drugs had become very serious problems.

But Brett fought hard against his troubles off the field and won, just as he has always fought hard on the field. Brett has proven again and again that he's a true champion. Those qualities helped Brett lead the Packers to two Super Bowls and become the first player to win three straight NFL Most Valuable Player awards.

"Brett is pure magic," Green Bay fullback William Henderson says. "When he's under pressure, he makes miracles happen."

BY THE BAYOU

The tiny Mississippi town of Kiln [KILL] is Brett Lorenzo Favre's hometown. When Brett was a kid, in the 1970s, Kiln had only 800 residents. Brett lived outside of town, in the country. That country upbringing is still with him. Once, wide receiver Andre Rison called him a hillbilly. Brett thanked him. "Because I am," Brett said.

Kiln sits next to a body of water called Rotten Bayou. Young Brett often skipped rocks across the bayou's alligator-infested water. The Favre family's dogs also played near the water. Three of them got a little too close: Alligators ate them.

Brett was like most kids. For example, he didn't like cleaning his room. He even slept on top of his sheets so that he didn't have to make the bed in the morning. He loved sports. His idols growing up were two quarterbacks for teams in the South: Roger Staubach of the Dallas Cowboys and Archie Manning of the New Orleans Saints. He dreamed of becoming a great NFL passer, just as they were.

AN ALL-AROUND ATHLETE

Brett soon proved to be a talented all-around athlete. At Hancock North Central High School, in Kiln, he earned a varsity letter every year in baseball and led his team in batting every season. He also earned three varsity letters for playing on the high school football team, which was coached by his father, Irvin. Brett could do many different things on the football field. At various times, he played quarterback, strong safety, punter, and placekicker. After his senior season, he was named to play on the Mississippi high school all-star team.

Brett wasn't the only talented athlete in his family. His dad had pitched for the University of Southern Mississippi varsity baseball team. Two of Brett's brothers played college football. Scott, who is one year older, was a quarterback at Mississippi State University. Jeff, four years younger, was a free safety for Southern Mississippi. Brett's sister, Brandi, excelled in another area: She earned the title of Miss Teen Mississippi.

In 1987, Brett entered the University of Southern Mississippi, the same college his dad attended. In only the third game of his freshman year, Brett became the football team's starting quarterback. In his college career, he set school records for the most touchdowns, completions, and passing yards, and for the highest passing percentage. Brett had an interception ratio of 1.57 (the number of interceptions per passes thrown). It was best among the 50 top-ranked college quarterbacks in the United States.

But on July 14, 1990, just before Brett's senior year, he was in a terrible car crash. He suffered a concussion, cuts, bruises, and a cracked vertebra. Three weeks later, doctors discovered that he had serious internal injuries, as well. Surgeons had to remove 30 inches of his intestines.

But Brett is tough. His recovery was surprisingly quick. He was back as starting quarterback only one month after the accident. He led his team to an upset over Alabama in his first game back, on September 8, 1990.

At the end of his senior year, Brett was named MVP of the 1990 All-American Bowl, a post-season bowl game. NFL scouts were impressed with his daring on the field and his missile-fast passes. After a scouting trip to watch Brett, a top official with one pro team said, "I just saw the NFL's next great quarterback."

Brett's pro career began soon afterward, but it wasn't so great. In April 1991, he was selected by the Atlanta Falcons in the second round of the NFL draft. In his first season, he was on the active roster (meaning he was eligible to play) for just three games. He played in two of them and attempted five passes without completing even one. Not the best start for an NFL quarterback.

Brett now admits that he messed things up in his early days as a pro. For one thing, he drank too much. He also didn't take the time to learn Atlanta's plays because, as a rookie, he thought he had little hope of playing. He didn't always show up when he was supposed to for team activities. Head Coach Jerry Glanville didn't like Brett's attitude.

One time, Coach Glanville fined Brett $1,500 for showing up late to a team photo session. "I got trapped behind a car wreck," Brett explained. The coach didn't buy this excuse. "Boy, you *are* a car wreck," he replied.

The next spring, Atlanta traded Brett to Green Bay for a first-round draft pick. Brett had not shown the Falcons much. They had no reason to think he would have a great career. Over the winter, Brett had gained weight. He was out of shape. His future didn't look good.

THROWING WILD

But Packer head coach Mike Holmgren recognized Brett's potential. Soon, the young passer got a chance to show what he could do. In the first quarter of the third game of the

BRETT'S BIO

Birth Date October 10, 1969

Height 6 feet 2 inches

Weight 220 lbs.

Homes Hattiesburg, Mississippi, and Green Bay, Wisconsin

College Major Special Education

Favorite Sports to Play (other than football) Basketball, golf, and fishing

Favorite Candy Bar Brett Favre MVP Bar

Favorite Dessert Cookies-and-cream ice cream

1992 season, Packer starting quarterback Don Majkowski got injured. The Packers needed someone to replace him. Coach Holmgren turned to Brett, and he came through dramatically. With just 13 seconds left, Brett launched a 35-yard touchdown pass to defeat the Cincinnati Bengals, 24–23.

Several years later, Brett admitted that he was lucky that first day. He said his performance was wild. "I should have thrown six or seven interceptions," Brett told *Sports Illustrated*. "I was throwing darts off guys' helmets, trying to throw the ball through people. I still didn't know the offense at all."

This had been a problem for Brett in Atlanta when he started out, and it remained a problem for him for a long time afterward. He didn't learn the complicated offenses used in the NFL. But somehow, he still was able to play well enough to remain the Packer starter. In fact, he made the Pro Bowl in 1992 and 1993. But Brett often ignored Green Bay's system. He was scrambling and throwing risky passes whenever plays didn't go smoothly. His frustrated coach often pleaded with him: "Let the system work for you!"

By early in the 1994 season, the Packer coaches were tired of Brett's inconsistency. A talented back-up quarterback, Mark Brunell, sat in the wings, waiting for his chance. Coach Holmgren asked each of his assistants who he believed should start as the Packers' passer. Mark got more votes than Brett.

But Coach Holmgren wasn't so sure. He thought for a while before reaching his decision. He chose Brett. Coach Holmgren could tell how talented Brett was. It troubled the coach that Brett was wasting all that talent. He called Brett into his office

"It's just you and me, buddy," Mr. Holmgren told him. "We're joined at the hip. Either we're going to the Super Bowl together or we're going down together."

A CHANGED MAN

Brett couldn't believe it. He had been sure that the coach was ready to bench him. This great vote of confidence was exactly what Brett needed. "Just hearing Mike say that saved me," he recalled later.

Brett was a new quarterback after that meeting with Coach Holmgren. He started using the Packer system instead of just making it up as he went along. He fired 24 touchdown passes over the rest of the season, with only seven interceptions. He also came in second in the MVP balloting, behind Steve Young of the San Francisco 49ers.

Brett's real glory years began in 1995. During that season, he led the Packers to the NFC championship game and was named the NFL's Most Valuable Player. He threw 38 TD passes. Only one NFL quarterback had ever thrown more in a single season. (It was Dan Marino of the Miami Dolphins, and he did it twice — throwing 48 touchdown passes in 1984, and 44 in 1986.) Brett also was chosen as starting quarterback in the Pro Bowl.

But Brett had a huge problem in his personal life by this time. He had become addicted to a painkiller called Vicodin. Over the years, he had suffered dozens of injuries playing football. He had had some major operations, but he didn't want to stop playing. So, he was given prescriptions for the pills to dull his pain.

But after awhile, he wasn't taking the pills just to kill the pain. Brett started to think that Vicodin actually sharpened his quarterback talents. He took more of the pills than he should have and at times when he really didn't need them. This was a big mistake. In February 1996, while he was in the hospital for ankle surgery, Brett experienced a seizure. His body shook uncontrollably as his arms, legs, and head flailed wildly. It was scary.

Soon, Brett learned that Vicodin might well have caused the seizure. That made him realize that he had a terrible addiction. For help, he entered a special rehabilitation clinic for 45 days. He held a press conference before he entered the clinic and told the world about his problem. He also assured everyone that his addiction to pills was over for good.

Brett was drug-free by the start of the 1996 season, and he was playing better than ever. He had his best season yet. He connected for 39 touchdown passes. He rushed for 136 yards and two more touchdowns. Brett was a Pro Bowl starter again and took home his second straight MVP award.

It was a great season for Green Bay, too. The Packers had once been a mighty football dynasty. They won Super Bowl I and Super Bowl II in 1967 and 1968. But 28 years went by without another NFL championship. Brett's brilliant quarterbacking helped end that drought at last.

Super Bowl XXXI (for the 1996 season) was played in New Orleans, a Louisiana city only about one hour from Brett's hometown. Many family members and friends planned to be at the Superdome, where the Packers would meet the New England Patriots. Brett was very excited. But then he came down with a flu bug in the days leading up to the game and could hardly drag himself out of bed. He could only practice a short time.

"I was worried," Brett said. "I waited my whole life to play in [the Super Bowl], and now I wasn't going to be healthy."

On Super Bowl Sunday, Brett woke up feeling ready to take on the Patriots. He was still sick, but he felt he could play. And play he did. He made two long touchdown passes, to Andre Rison and Antonio Freeman. He scored another TD himself by barreling in from the two-yard line. Brett helped the Packers beat the Patriots, 35–21.

"It would be great to win anywhere," a grinning Brett told reporters after the game. "But being so close to home . . . I don't believe this could be better." Packer fans were delighted, too. They finally had their third championship.

The 1997 season was another great one for Brett. He led the NFL in touchdown passes, with 35, and became the first NFL quarterback to throw 30 or more TDs in four straight seasons. Here's another impressive stat: Brett connected for more touchdown passes in a four-season span than anyone in NFL history except the Dolphins' Dan Marino.

Most important of all, Brett led the Packers back to the Super Bowl, in January 1998. This time, they ran into superstar John Elway and a determined Denver Bronco team and lost, 31–24. But Brett stung the Broncos for three TDs and 256 yards. He shared regular-season MVP honors with Barry Sanders, the great Detroit Lion running back.

The 1998 season turned into something of a disappointment for Brett. After three outstanding seasons and two trips to the Super Bowl, he and the Packers just didn't quite have the same success. The team was upset by the San Francisco 49ers, 30–27, during the first round of the playoffs in the NFC. During the regular season, Brett threw more interceptions than he had since 1993 — 23 of them.

Brett began to realize that he couldn't be young and great forever. In May 1999, Brett told *Sports Illustrated* that he was concerned about his future. "I'll be thirty this year, and I don't want to be the forgotten man," he said.

Brett would be pretty hard to forget. For one thing, he put up some great numbers during the 1998 season. He completed 347 passes for 4,212 yards and 31 TDs. He started all 16 regular-season games for the sixth straight year.

Most important, though, Brett had left some bad habits behind and found new meaning in his world. Instead of going out a lot, partying, and drinking too much, he had become a family man. "I've lived a fun, hard life," Brett said. "But fun now is watching [my daughter] Brittany play softball. Fun is having rookies in the weight room look at me as an example of what they want to be. I'm done with alcohol."

In July 1999, Brett's wife, Deanna, gave birth to another daughter, Breleigh Ann. "He was pretty excited," Brett's mother told reporters. "He just kept smiling and saying, 'She's daddy's little girl.'"

ROLLING ON

The Packers slipped to 8–8 in the 1999 season, but Brett had another solid showing. He completed 341 of a league-leading 595 pass attempts for 4,091 yards. Once again Brett started all 16 Green Bay games. In September, he was named the NFC Player of the Month after throwing for 925 yards and five TDs in three games. In two of the games, Brett led the Pack to come-from-behind victories.

Green Bay rebounded to a 9-7 record in 2000. For the eighth consecutive year, Brett started every game. Brett led the NFC with 580 pass attempts, completing 338 of them.

In February 2001, Brett signed a lifetime contract with the Packers, almost assuring that he will finish his career in Green Bay. Packer general manager and head coach Mike Sherman called Brett's signing "historic." "I do not think there is a player in the NFL that experiences a relationship with the fans like Brett Favre does. That's very, very special," said Coach Sherman.

A GIVING GUY

In 1996, Brett started the Brett Favre Forward Foundation, which raises hundreds of thousands of dollars for charities through an annual golf tournament.

Brett also has brought in a lot of cash for the Boys & Girls Club of Green Bay. How? He donates $150 for each TD he scores by passing or rushing. Even better, he has arranged for several corporations to match his donations. Altogether, these contributions totaled $164,000 for the Boys & Girls Club in 1998 alone.

The Packers reemerged as one of the league's top teams in 2001, posting a 12–4 record. Brett had another solid season, throwing for 3,921 yards and 32 TDs. Green Bay beat San Francisco in the wild–card playoff game, 25–15, but got clobbered by the St. Louis Rams, 45–17, in the division title game. Brett threw six interceptions in the disappointing loss. But Green Bay's strong 2001 performance behind their 32-year old quarterback put everyone on notice that they were back — and aiming for another shot at a Super Bowl victory.

FOR THE RECORD

Brett's career performance has him on a sure path to the NFL Hall of Fame. In addition to his three straight MVPs and the Super Bowl win, take a look at some of Brett's career highlights going into the 2002 season:

• Brett tops all NFL quarterbacks in completions, pass attempts, passing yards, and TDs in the decade of 1991–2000.

• Brett is the only quarterback in NFL history to throw for 3,000 yards in 11 straight seasons.

• Brett owns the NFL record for quarterbacks by starting 157 consecutive games.

• Brett has 30-touchdown seasons — the most in NFL history.

BRETT GOES HOLLYWOOD

Brett is a good-looking guy and he isn't exactly camera-shy. He has acted in a major Hollywood movie. Brett made a brief appearance near the end of the 1998 film *There's Something About Mary*. The movie starred actress Cameron Diaz as Mary, and was a big success. In 1997, Brett appeared in *Reggie's Prayer*, a film put together by his former Green Bay teammate Reggie White. Brett has also been a guest on many national TV shows, including "The Tonight Show with Jay Leno" and "The Late Show with David Letterman."

Brett is not shy about talking about his hopes. "In my mind, I think I can be the best ever. That's my goal, to be the best. I don't know if that will ever happen, but I think it's important to set high goals," Brett wrote in his autobiography, *For the Record*. "I want someone to write a book someday and say, 'That Brett Favre was the greatest quarterback of all time. He could do it all.'"

A ROLE MODEL AT LAST

Brett Favre has come a long way. He now understands his responsibilities to himself, to his family, to his team — and to others. "I'm getting a lot of letters from parents and teachers telling me I'm a role model, which is something I never thought I'd be," Brett told *Time* magazine. "And some people are writing to tell me I've given them the courage to face their own problems. That's not why I stopped [drinking], to be an inspiration. But if I help people while I'm helping myself, that's okay."

>> KOBE BRYANT

Young and talented, this guard made a great leap to the NBA

The game is on the line, and the Los Angeles Lakers need help. It's January 19, 1998, the Lakers are playing the Orlando Magic in L.A.'s Great Western Forum. With just a little time left, the Lakers lead by only one point. The Lakers could use some anti–Magic magic to ensure the victory.

Laker forward Robert Horry tries to make it happen. He stands at the free throw line, concentrating hard before he arcs his shot toward the backboard. He misses. He shoots again. The ball bounces off, and it looks like no score for the Lakers. *Wait.* The play isn't over. Twisting his body like a cat, guard Kobe Bryant instantly slips in front of Danny Schayes of the Magic. Kobe is playing in only his second NBA season, but he reaches up, as if he has been doing this forever, and taps the ball lightly. Two points! Kobe's dazzling move puts the Lakers up by three.

It was not to last. With 22 seconds left, two Orlando free throws make the score 89–88. Laker guard Nick Van Exel

is fouled immediately, but makes only one free throw. The score is now 90–88. With the clock running down, Magic forward Horace Grant is fouled. As the opposing teams line up for the foul shots, the Magic's Derek Harper looks at Kobe and lays some trash talk on the 19-year-old kid. "Let a veteran show you how to knock down a couple of free throws," Derek razzes.

Talk is cheap, though, and Derek and his teammates soon find themselves scrambling after Horace misses his second shot. L.A. still leads, 90–89. Orlando is forced to commit a quick foul to stop the clock. Worse yet: They have no choice except to foul Kobe.

"Let a young fella show you how to do it," Kobe teases back as he takes the ball to the free throw line. There are just 7.7 seconds left to play in the game as Kobe gazes at the basket. Coolly and cleanly, he sinks first one shot and then the second to ice the 92–89 victory for Los Angeles. Once again, the cool kid has shown the tough veterans just what he can do with a basketball in his hands.

CAN-DO KOBE

Kobe Bryant is truly an amazing young player. How many athletes — in any sport — go straight from high school to the big time, as he did? How many are almost instantly compared to the greatest star their sport has ever known? How many can withstand the pressure that comes along with being "the next Michael Jordan" and still deliver when it counts? Kobe can.

Game after game since joining the NBA in 1996, Kobe has proved that his talent is the real thing. By his third season (1998–99), at the age of only 20, he was regarded as one of the best players in the league. Listen to one of his teammates: "Hey, next time he does something . . . take your eyes off Kobe, if you can, and you look at the Laker bench," suggests Robert Horry. "We're over there going, *'Oh-hhh-hhh!'* just like everybody else. The stuff he does is incredible."

A EUROPEAN EDUCATION

Kobe was born to shoot a basketball. His father, Joe "Jelly Bean" Bryant, played in the NBA for eight years. Joe specialized in defense, coming off the bench to guard the opposing team's best players. He played for several teams, but he started out with the Philadelphia 76ers. He was part of the Philly team that made it all the way to the 1977 NBA Finals.

Kobe was born a year later, on August 23, 1978, in Philadelphia. He was the youngest child and the only son in the family. He has two older sisters, Sharia and Shaya. His mother's name is Pamela. After Joe's NBA career ended, in 1984, he packed up with Pam and the three kids for a true adventure. The Bryants moved to Rieti, Italy, so that Joe could continue playing pro basketball. This turned out to be a very important event in Kobe's life.

Kobe started school in Europe. He was six years old, entering the first grade. His sisters were entering second and third grades. None of the Bryant children spoke Italian, so they had to work like crazy just to get their education.

"My two sisters and I got together after school to teach one another the words we had learned," Kobe recalled. "I was able to speak Italian pretty well within a few months." Kobe remembers eating lots of pasta and walking through the Alps mountains with his family on Saturdays.

The Bryants lived in Italy for eight years, but it wasn't all lasagna and Alps. Because he was the son of a basketball player, Kobe learned to play basketball, too — even though soccer was the most popular sport for Italian kids. "After school, I would be the only guy on the basketball court, working on my moves," Kobe said.

LEARNING BY WATCHING

Kobe also was able to do some things that he would not have done had he lived in the United States. Kobe often practiced beside his father's team after school. He even shot baskets during halftime at the team's games. The crowd cheered him on, and Kobe loved it.

Then there were the videotapes. Kobe's grandparents back in the United States taped the best NBA games and mailed off the videos every couple of days. Kobe and his dad watched them together as Dad explained what was happening on the court and why it was happening. Kobe replayed those tapes many times, memorizing the plays and learning from the stars of the NBA. Kobe and his dad especially enjoyed videos of the Laker games. They watched videos of about 40 Los Angeles games a year. Kobe was already a Laker fan. He even had worn a small Laker team jacket as a baby.

Kobe says those videotapes helped him learn to play the way he does today. "My baseline jumper, I got it from [Hall of Fame guard] Oscar Robertson," he told *Sports Illustrated.* "Oscar liked to use his size against smaller players. That's what I try to do." Kobe said his fall away jump shot came from copying center Hakeem Olajuwon of the Houston Rockets, now with the Toronto Raptors. He learned from Earl "the Pearl" Monroe how to "shake one way, then go back the other way." Earl was a brilliant ball handler.

In 1992, the Bryants returned to the United States and lived in Philadelphia. Kobe was 14. He soon joined a summer basketball league in Philadelphia. On his league application, Kobe wrote that his future career would be in the NBA. A counselor scolded him for it. "The guy said NBA players are one in a million," he recalled. "I said, 'Man, look, I'm going to be that one in a million.'"

PLAYER OF THE YEAR

The boy began proving his point before long. At Lower Merion High School, in Ardmore, Pennsylvania, Kobe was the star. He was a starter during all four years. In his final three seasons, he helped the team to a 77–13 record. *USA Today* and *Parade* magazine picked Kobe as the National High School Player of the Year during his senior season.

Kobe was 6 feet 5 inches tall and averaged more than 30 points a game — thanks in part to some serious slam-dunking skills. Kobe also led his team to a state title that season. He was awesome. He was so famous that when he announced that he wanted to take the singer Brandy to his prom, she accepted.

After all this success, then what? Most high school stars go to college and delay joining the NBA for a few years. Hardly anybody had gone straight to the pros. But Kobe wasn't anybody. Sure, he was a solid B student in school who could have gone to a good university and played in one of the best college basketball programs. But he didn't do that.

Instead, Kobe decided to join the world's best players . . . the National Basketball Association. It was quite a leap — from shooting against high school guys to taking on Michael Jordan. But Kobe, his parents, and his coach all thought he could do it. And so did some NBA teams.

The Charlotte Hornets chose Kobe as the 13th overall pick in 1996, then traded him that same day to Los Angeles. The kid was going to play for the team he had always loved. He also was going to work for one of his idols: former Laker superstar Magic Johnson. Magic had retired as a player in 1991 and had become a Laker vice president.

"It's like God blessed that trade so that Kobe could come out here and be around a guy who can help him by sitting and watching him every night," Magic said. "I'm going to take care of him. But I'm also going to criticize him when he has to be criticized."

Kobe began to live his dream. He was playing for the Lakers — and Magic Johnson was watching *him* instead of the other way around. Kobe even has Magic's old locker.

ALL-STAR KOBE

Kobe's first season, 1996–97, was respectable for a rookie. He played in 71 games, starting six times and averaging nearly eight points per game. On January 28, 1997, in Dallas, Kobe became the youngest player ever to start an NBA game. After the season, he was selected for the NBA All-Rookie Second Team.

During the 1997–98 season, Kobe really began to show his talents. Though he started only once, he played in 79 games and established himself as the Lakers' valuable "sixth man." The sixth man is the first player to come off the bench to substitute for one of the starters. A good sixth man is as valuable as a starter. Kobe certainly was valuable to the Lakers. He scored in double-figures (10 or more points) in 65 games. One time he scored 27 points in less than 13 minutes.

In February 1998, Kobe became the youngest All-Star in NBA history. He started for the Western Conference at the age of 19 years, five months, and 16 days. Kobe was hyped as Michael Jordan's big rival in that All-Star Game. A full-page newspaper ad pictured these two players alone, face to face. "I said, 'Cool,'" Kobe says. "It was like they were making it out to be some big one-on-one showdown."

Kobe responded well to the pressure. He scored 18 points, the highest individual total for the Western squad. Kobe also showed up on all the highlight tapes after making the most awesome play of the game: a behind-the-back dribble that ended with a breakaway slam dunk. Showtime!

The next season was upset by the NBA players strike. Still, Kobe continued to improve. He played in all 50 of the team's games in the strike–shortened regular season. He averaged nearly 20 points per game and led the Lakers in scoring in 11 games. Once, he scored 38 points in a game — 33 of them in the second half. Kobe banged the boards too. He put together nine double–doubles for the year (scoring 10 or more points and 10 or more rebounds).

After the season, Kobe was named to the 1998–99 All–NBA Third Team. The comparisons with Michael Jordan kept coming. One of these came from a pretty good source — Phil Jackson, who had coached Michael with the Chicago Bulls. The Lakers hired Coach Jackson in June 1999 to run their team. Guess what he told reporters? He said that Kobe reminded him of Michael.

By then, Kobe was so well–known that he had his own line of sneakers — and they were selling well. He was making a lot of money from the Lakers and from endorsing other products. But all the fame and money didn't seem to go to Kobe's head. He still lived with his parents and sisters, in a house he bought. His mother cooked for him, but Kobe did his own laundry. When asked what he liked to do after a game, Kobe said: "I go home with my mother, my father, or my sisters. We have a nice little dinner together. Then I go to sleep."

Kobe is no boring guy, though. He writes poetry and has recorded a hip–hop song. He also likes to have fun. He kids around with fans and even with the various reporters

MUSICAL MOVES

Some observers have said that great basketball stars move with the grace of ballet dancers. Julius Erving and Michael Jordan were two of the best ever to leap above a basketball court. But how many big-time basketball stars have made a hip-hop record? Kobe has.

R&B singer Brian McKnight asked him to join in the remix of the song "Hold Me." The cut was recorded and released during the NBA's off-season in 1999. The pair also made a video together. But Kobe said there is no solo CD in his future — at least not yet.

"Right now, I'm too busy playing basketball to begin a serious recording career. Ball is my focus now," he told fans.

who cover basketball. One day, a reporter remarked that he sometimes wore Kobe's signature shoes.

"Oh, yeah? How do you like them?" Kobe asked, smiling.

"Well, whatever plastic they use makes the shoes smell, and I have to keep them out in the garage," the reporter replied.

"You ever try changing your socks?" Kobe joked with a grin. The reporters laughed and high-fived after that one.

People expect a lot from Kobe on the basketball court. They will probably keep expecting a lot from him for a long time. That's okay. Kobe expects a great deal from himself, too. When the game clock is running, he's deadly serious. He takes the ball, then spins, whirls, soars, and slams. It's what "the next Jordan" is expected to do.

But Kobe is smart enough to enjoy himself as he lives his lifelong dream of NBA stardom. He takes basketball seriously, but he doesn't take himself too seriously. "I feel like a kid, and sometimes I feel like a grownup," Kobe said. "I have the best of both worlds."

A CHAMP

All that seemed to be missing from Kobe's world was The Big Prize — an NBA championship. Coach Jackson had the experience to turn the Lakers from a contending team into a winner. In the 1999-2000 season, he got the Lakers to play as a team. With Shaquille O'Neal as the big man in the middle and Kobe running the offense, the Lakers stormed through the season. Kobe put up career-high numbers of 22.5 points, 4.9 assists, and 6.3 rebounds per game. In the NBA Finals against the Indiana Pacers, Kobe had the game-winning overtime basket in Game 4. In Game 6, Kobe knocked in 26 points, as the Lakers captured their first NBA title since 1988.

One of the hardest things to do in professional sports is to win consecutive championships. In the early part of the 2000-01 season, the Lakers were learning that lesson the hard way. Los Angeles lost their first three pre-season games. Many people began to wonder what was wrong. Some people blamed Kobe for taking too many shots and not looking to pass off to his teammates. Shaq agreed with those people.

Coach Jackson worked hard to settle the tensions in the Laker locker room, getting his team to focus on playing better basketball. Coach Jackson's magic seemed to work as the Lakers began to dominate their opponents as they had in the previous season.

BOXFUL OF BRYANT

Birth Date August 23, 1978

Height 6 foot 7 inches

Weight 210 lbs.

Home Pacific Palisades, California

College None, but he has taken courses at the University of California at Los Angeles

Favorite Sport to Play (other than basketball) Soccer

Favorite Sport to Watch (other than basketball) Tennis

Favorite Foods Lasagna and apple pie

Favorite Athletes Football players Barry Sanders and Emmitt Smith

Favorite Hobby "Dancing. I love all types of dancing."

Place He Would Most Like to Visit North Pole

THE NAME GAME

Kobe is an unusual first name. But it's not so unusual if you're a piece of beef. The young Laker star got his name from a special cut of Japanese steak. Kobe beef are steaks from special cows that live in the area of Kobe, Japan. His parents spotted the word on a menu at a steak house and liked the sound it made: Ko - beee! Mr. Bryant recalled that the restaurant was located in King of Prussia, Pennsylvania. "But I don't know if I should say that," Kobe's dad added, "because they might want the rights to his name!"

Kobe played outstanding ball once again. In December 2000, he was chosen the NBA Player of the Month by averaging 32.3 points, 4.8 rebounds, and 4.9 assists per game. Kobe received the most votes for his position in the All–Star voting. In the 2001 All–Star Game, Kobe led his Western Conference teammates with 19 points and seven assists in a 111–110 losing effort to the Eastern Conference all–stars.

Kobe ended the season with even more career highs. He averaged 28.5 points and five assists per game. On one memorable night, he scored a career-high 51 points against the Golden State Warriors.

The Lakers roared through the playoffs with their eyes set on a repeat championship performance. In the first round of playoffs, they swept the Portland Trail Blazers. In the conference semifinals, they swept the Sacramento Kings. In the conference finals, they swept the 1999–2000 champion San Antonio Spurs. The Lakers had won 11 straight playoff games.

The Lakers last obstacle was the Philadelphia 76ers and their star guard, Allen Iverson, in the NBA Finals. After a surprising upset win by the 76ers in Game 1, the Lakers took control and never looked back. In Game 5, Kobe scored 26 to help the Lakers take the series, 4–1. The Lakers posted an astonishing 15–1 record in the playoffs. Kobe was a huge reason for his team's success. He had averaged 24.6 points, 7.8 rebounds, and 5.8 assists per game in the Finals.

As he's become one of today's hottest young athletes, Kobe has grown as a player and person. Everyone noticed it. Coach Jackson said, "I think he's mature beyond his years . . . I think he's grown a lot . . ."

Kobe's philosophy is simple. "Basketball is kind of like life. You can get knocked on your butt. But you have to get up and hold your head high and try again. That's how I'm going to be."

>> TIM DUNCAN

Dunkin' is what this guy does for a living, and how

He's a cool one, this Tim Duncan. The San Antonio Spurs' young star is a very cool customer on the basketball court. Let other players wag their tongues, growl, or shriek. Tim simply plays the game. Let Allen Iverson create spine-tingling drama. Let Shaquille O'Neal demonstrate heavy-duty intensity with a back-board-shaking slam. Just give Tim a chance to do his thing with the ball, and then watch.

He can do his thing, all right. In 1997–98, his rookie season, the 7-foot forward proved that he could do nearly everything on the court, offensively and defensively. He averaged 21.1 points, 11.9 rebounds, and 2.51 blocks per game to earn the NBA Rookie of the Year award. The next season, Tim won something even more important: the NBA playoff finals Most Valuable Player award.

Tim's most famous teammate, center David Robinson, was quite impressed after playing with Tim during only one season. "If Michael Jordan retires," David said in 1998, "then Tim is about the best player in the league."

Well, Michael Jordan — the King of the Court — did retire, in January 1999. (Michael returned to NBA action, playing for the Washington Wizards in the 2001–02 season.) In June 1999, Tim helped the Spurs win the NBA title, which had belonged to Michael and his Chicago Bulls. Maybe it is time to crown a new, laidback ruler of the hoops. Maybe Tim Duncan will be the new King of the Court.

HURRICANE FORCE

Tim comes from a tropical island in the Caribbean Sea, which is southeast of Florida. He was born on April 25, 1976, on the island of St. Croix [CROY]. St. Croix is part of the United States Virgin Islands. It is a beautiful island, but very small. The population is about 55,000, which is roughly the size of a small U.S. city. Tim lived there with his mom, Ione, his dad, William, and his two sisters, Cheryl and Tricia.

As a kid, Tim never imagined becoming a great basketball star. No, he wanted to become a great Olympic swimmer. His older sister, Tricia, was an excellent swimmer. She competed in swimming at the 1988 Summer Olympic Games, in Seoul, South Korea. Tim wanted to be a great swimmer like Tricia. He might have made it, too. When he was only 13 years old, he was among the best of the U.S. kids in his age group at swimming the 400–meter freestyle. He seemed to be on track to make the Olympic team.

Then disaster struck — for real. In 1989, a huge natural disaster changed Tim's life. Hurricane Hugo roared through St. Croix that year. The storm was so powerful it damaged about 80 percent of the buildings on the island. Hugo also wiped out the only Olympic-size pool there. Tim had no place to train.

That wasn't the worst of it. Tim's mother, Ione, had been ill when the hurricane hammered St. Croix. She was fighting a fierce battle against breast cancer. She needed regular chemotherapy treatments to survive. But when Hugo hit the island, the furious wind and water knocked

TIM'S TALE

Birth Date August 25, 1976

Height 7 feet

Weight 255 lbs.

Homes San Antonio, Texas, and St. Croix, U.S. Virgin Islands

Favorite Sport to Play (other than basketball) Football

Favorite Athlete Former basketball great Magic Johnson

Favorite Food Steak

Favorite Music Reggae

Favorite Book *Jurassic Park*, by Michael Crichton

Biggest Fears Sharks and high places; "Luckily, I don't have to face either one of them in the NBA," Tim points out.

out electricity all over St. Croix. With hospitals and roads damaged and power outages that lasted as long as two months, Mrs. Duncan couldn't receive her cancer treatments in a timely way. The cancer overwhelmed her and she died seven months after the storm hit.

DISASTER AND DEVASTATION

As you can imagine, Tim was devastated by the death of his mother. Hurricane Hugo had destroyed large parts of his world. His Olympic dreams were also dead. What was left for him? What could he do?

First, Tim did what anyone would do. He grieved over the loss of his mother. Tim also felt disappointment over his swimming future. Eventually, though, Tim picked himself up and started to move on with his life. He found a new sport to throw his energies into: basketball.

Tim played organized basketball for the first time in the ninth grade. He played at St. Dunstan's Episcopal High School, in Christiansted, a port city in St. Croix. His talents developed quickly. Soon Tim was one of the most impressive, dominating players on the island.

Still, St. Croix is off the beaten track. College basketball coaches don't visit regularly looking for players with potential. But as it happened, in 1992, a group of young NBA players visited St. Croix to promote their league. One rookie, Chris King, had played at Wake Forest University, in Winston–Salem, North Carolina. Chris saw Tim playing in St. Croix. He persuaded Wake Forest coach Dave Odom to check out this talented kid. Tim was just 16.

Soon, other schools heard about Tim, too. They wanted Tim to play for them. But Tim eventually settled on Wake Forest and started school there, in 1993.

At Wake Forest, Tim became one of the best college players in the country. He won the important Naismith and Wooden awards. He was named the 1996–97 NCAA National Player of the Year by the Associated Press, the U.S. Basketball Writers, the *Sporting News*, the National Association of Basketball Coaches, and others. The Associated Press named him a First Team All-America.

And no wonder. Look at some of the things he did on the court: Tim blocked 481 shots to become the all-time leading shot-blocker in Atlantic Coast Conference history and second all-time in the entire NCAA. He was the first college player to score more than 1,500 points, grab more than 1,000 rebounds, block more than 400 shots, *and* pass for more than 200 assists in a career. He helped Wake Forest become the first team in 14 years to win back-to-back ACC championships. Pretty amazing stuff.

Nearly everyone thought that Tim would leave college after his junior year and join the NBA. He could easily have been the number one draft pick. But he didn't. When his mother was dying, she had made Tim and his sisters promise to earn college diplomas. Tim didn't want to break that promise. So he stayed at Wake Forest and graduated with a degree in psychology. His sisters also kept their promises to their mom.

SLAMMIN' FOR CHARITY

Tim is a good guy, even off the court. He works actively with the Spurs Foundation, which benefits the United Way and the Children's Bereavement Center of San Antonio. The center assists children who lose a parent, as Tim did. He also donates 25 tickets to each home game so that kids who can't afford tickets may watch the Spurs live.

Tim also helps out NBA Team Up, an organization that encourages young people to improve their community. And he is looking for ways to take sports and business opportunities to St. Croix.

BATMAN AND ROBIN

After Tim graduated, the San Antonio Spurs chose him as the number one pick in the 1997 NBA draft. Getting Tim was a great move for the Spurs. They had finished sixth in their division in the 1996–97 season. They needed something more, and Tim was that something.

Tim had played center throughout high school and college. The Spurs already had a terrific center in David Robinson. Two centers on one team could have caused problems. But the coaches were smart enough to play Tim at forward, alongside David, who is 10 years older and much more experienced. That gave the team two tall, strong, talented men battling opponents side by side — the young rookie and the mighty veteran. They are sort of like Batman and Robin — only they're both tall.

Tim and David quickly became an effective combination against even the best teams. This double-trouble strategy worked because Tim and David found ways to work together. They became good friends, too. Right after the 1997 NBA draft, David invited Tim to his home near Aspen, Colorado. Together they lifted weights and played one-on-one, with David offering advice and Tim listening.

"I've tried to help Tim understand that if you don't prepare yourself, you don't perform well," David said. Only halfway through his new buddy's rookie year, David announced that he would rather play with Tim than with any forward in the Western Conference, including veteran All-Star Karl Malone of the Utah Jazz.

Tim had a great first season. He was the only rookie selected for the 1998 All-Star Game. He won Rookie of the Month during each of the season's six months. And he received 113 of 116 votes in the NBA Rookie of the Year voting.

MR. MODEST

Tim's performance during the 1997–98 season justified all the awards, just as it had during his college career. He led the NBA with 57 double-doubles (games in which he gets 10 or more of two of the following: points, rebounds, blocks, assists, or steals). Tim scored in double figures 77 times, including fifty 20-point games and eight 30-point efforts. Tim was also among the NBA leaders in scoring, rebounding, shot-blocking, and field-goal percentage.

Through his success, Tim remained modest. When a fan asked about his transition to pro basketball, he said:

"It's been a long season that has been tough at times. But I've had a lot of help, so it has been great. I'm learning, but I have a long way to go." He also gave David plenty of credit for offering advice and lessons during that rookie year.

People sometimes criticized Tim because of his laid-back manner. But Tim's cool style obviously works just fine on a basketball court. It doesn't mean that Tim lacks feelings, or isn't trying, or that he doesn't laugh and have fun. Far from it. He sometimes wears his practice shorts backward, for instance. And he has two tattoos: a magician and a wizard. Tim keeps others loose when they're on the road.

"He busts into my room on road trips and, if there's a basketball game on, he makes me turn to wrestling," recalled Antonio Daniels, a Spur guard and Tim's best friend. "We're in each other's rooms hours a day, watching TV and laughing."

One other little-known fact about Tim: He is the Spurs' video-game champion. Forward Sean Elliott (who has since retired) had been the team's undisputed video king — until he invited a rookie named Tim Duncan to his house.

"You have to understand, I don't lose at home. I'm King Video. When the neighborhood kids come around to play, I make it a point to destroy them," Sean said. "None of the other guys on the team can come close to me. But then this rookie comes along and he humbles me. He made me go out and buy a game manual so I can study the moves more." In Tim's own home, he has so much video-game equipment, it doesn't all fit into one room.

But life isn't all video games for Tim. He works hard at basketball. Even after his astounding rookie season, he

NAME THAT STAR

By late 1999, fans and players were still looking for the right nickname for Tim. David Robinson, who attended the U.S. Naval Academy, is called "the Admiral." Should Tim be "the General" or what? One former teammate, Mario Elie, called Tim either "the Big Easy" or "the Quiet Assassin." "Merlin" is another nickname.

Even Tim's official website at www.slamduncan.com was looking for just the right nickname. The website asked fans to choose among "the Big Easy", "the Cruzan Illusion", "Cash Flow", and "Magnum V.I."

But we think they might have missed the best name of all, even if it is a bit obvious. How about "Slam Duncan"?

worked hard. He understood that work was the only way to keep the sharp edge on his talent. His pal David Robinson knew this, too. Following the strike that shortened the 1998–99 season by 32 games, Tim and David were two of only three players with contracts who showed up for the Spurs' first voluntary workout. This was after almost eight months away from the game.

Once official competition finally got underway, Tim's pre-season efforts really paid off. With David at his side, he helped make 1999 a memorable year for San Antonio fans, at last. The Spurs had a reputation as a team with talent, just not quite enough talent to make it all the way.

For 10 years, they had struggled to get into the NBA Finals. Each year they somehow fell short. This was a huge frustration for all the Spurs, especially David.

But with Tim in his second season with the team, things finally changed. He put up high individual numbers, just as he had during his rookie year. He was the only NBA player who ranked among the Top 10 in each of these categories: scoring (sixth), rebounding (fifth), blocked shots (seventh), and field–goal percentage (eighth).

What's more, he showed himself to be capable of coming up with a really Big Game. For example, in April 1999, he scored a career–high 39 points in a 103–91 win over the Vancouver Grizzlies. Tim sank 13 of those points in the third quarter alone. He also had 13 rebounds and six blocked shots in the game. That kind of huge performance can be key during the playoffs.

TITLE-BOUND

The Spurs rolled through the regular season and into the NBA Finals for the first time. There they faced the New York Knicks. The Knicks had a problem: Their best player, All–Star center Patrick Ewing, was out with a serious injury. But they had two even bigger problems: Tim and David were healthy.

With San Antonio leading the Finals series three games to one, the fifth game grew tense. New York was battling to keep its season alive. Tim and David had used their size and skill all game long to control the basket, offensively and defensively. But with little time left to play, the Spurs were ahead by only one point. The Knicks could still win and avoid elimination.

There were just 2.1 seconds left on the clock. The Knicks had the ball and threw it inbounds to Latrell Sprewell, who was standing under the basket. Latrell tried hard to break free for a good shot. Against most teams, he would have succeeded, too. But not against the Spurs, with Tim and David ganging up on him. An instant later, the final buzzer sounded. The Knicks' last-ditch effort to score had failed. San Antonio had won, 78–77. They were the NBA champions.

A NEW KING

Tim was brilliant in that NBA Finals series. He had 27.4 points, 14 rebounds, and 2.1 blocked shots per game to earn the Finals MVP trophy. Shortly after the decisive game, David wrote a story for *Sports Illustrated*. "It's also a great feeling to have Tim Duncan by my side," David wrote. "He's obviously the best player in the league. Tim was phenomenal against New York, and his Finals MVP award was well-deserved."

A year earlier, David had said Tim might become "the best player in the league." Now he was convinced. Tim had risen to the top with his overwhelming display during the Finals.

SEASON-ENDING INJURY

Tim carried the success of the Spurs' championship run into the 1999–2000 season. He finished the season with 23.2 points, 12.4 rebounds, 3.2 assists, and 2.2 blocked shots per game. He was only one of two players to rank among the top ten in scoring, rebounds, and blocks. Tim was named to the All–NBA First Team and the NBA All–Defensive First Team for the second straight season. He was also chosen as the co–MVP of the 2000 NBA All–Star Game, sharing the honor with Los Angeles Laker Shaquille O'Neal.

Tim played in only 74 of the Spurs' 82 games due to injuries. In late February and early March, he missed four games due to a lower stomach muscle strain. He made his way back into the lineup, but in a game against the Sacramento Kings on April 11, Tim tore the cartilage in his left knee. He missed the last four games of the regular season and the entire playoffs.

Tim did everything he could to return to playoff action, but his teammates didn't want him risking further injury by coming back to play too soon. "I know he's dying to play, but if you can't run, you can't play. It's just that simple," said David Robinson. Without Tim in the lineup, the Spurs were knocked out of the playoffs in the first round by the Phoenix Suns, 3–1.

On May 24, Tim had surgery to repair his knee.

BACK TO BUSINESS

In the off–season, Tim re–signed with the Spurs, to the happiness of his teammates and San Antonio fans. The Orlando Magic made a serious attempt to sign Tim, but when it was time to make a decision, Tim wanted to stick with the Spurs. "When it came down to it, I just liked what I had here," he said.

In good health all season, Tim turned in another out-standing season in 2000–01. He averaged 22.2 points, 12.2 rebounds, and three assists per game. For the third straight season, he made both the All–NBA First Team and the NBA All–Defensive First Team. With Tim leading the way, the Spurs rolled to a league–best 58–24 record.

In the Western Conference finals, the Spurs faced the Lakers, led by the powerhouse duo of Shaq and Kobe. Tim played well in the series, averaging 23.2 points and 12.3 rebounds per game, but the Lakers swept San Antonio in four games. Tim was disappointed, but gave credit to the way the Lakers played. "They played incredibly. They were better in the series [than the Spurs]; they always seemed to have an answer for us," Tim said.

TOWER OF GIVING

Tim's on–the–court excellence is matched by the work he does for others in his community.

In 2001, Tim was awarded the Home Team Community Service Award by the NBA and Fannie Mae Foundation, an organization dedicated to improving housing conditions. The award recognized Tim's help in rebuilding inner–city neighborhoods throughout the country.

Tim's sense of responsibility — on and off the court — has taken him a long way from being a child swimmer in St. Croix to one of the NBA's most respected stars.

NEWSFLASH! *Tim was named the NBA MVP in the 2001-02 season! He averaged 25.5 points and 12.7 rebounds per game.*

>> MIA HAMM

It isn't just love of the game that makes Mia great

Mia Hamm is all about hard work, dedication to winning, and love — love of soccer and love of her family. Mia's deep feelings for the game grew out of her even deeper feelings for her family. And, in turn, Mia's family memories help inspire her great play.

Those two parts of Mia's life came together in a single game after the death of her beloved older brother, Garrett. In 1997, Garrett died after years of fighting a rare blood disorder. He was just 28 years old. Garrett had been the reason Mia was drawn to soccer as a kid. He had helped give his sister the confidence she needed to compete successfully as a young athlete. But now Garrett was gone.

At the time Garrett died, Mia was playing in the U.S. Women's Soccer Team's victory tour. She missed two games after Garrett died. Then Mia decided the best way to honor her brother was to pull herself together as much as possible and play soccer. It was what he would have wanted her to do. So Mia rejoined the

team, in Tampa, Florida. She arrived just in time for matches against the team from South Korea.

The first game was played in heavy rain. Despite the weather, there was a sellout crowd that included Garrett's widow, Cherylynn.

Mia was playing the game for Garrett. She wanted to play her best. Unknown to Mia, her teammates had decided to attach black armbands to their uniforms in memory of Garrett. When Mia saw this thoughtful gesture by her friends, she was deeply moved. By the time the game started, Mia was feeling so many emotions. One had to wonder how she could play at all. But she did — and how.

INSPIRED BY GARRETT

Mia is a forward, known for her quick moves and lightning speed down the field. Playing for Garrett inspired her and she quickly seized control of the game. Only 49 seconds into the match, Mia scored her first goal.

Seventeen minutes later, she scored again. When all was said and done, Mia was on the field for 54 of the game's 60 minutes, despite the torrential rain. Her two early goals had sparked the team to a 7–0 victory. Mia had given her best, just as she had hoped to do.

Later, she explained that something had felt different during the game. Mia said she knew that someone she loved and missed terribly was watching over her. It was a feeling that she would have every time she stepped onto a soccer field after that. "Now, no matter where I play, I feel Garrett is there," she said.

Mia is arguably the best soccer player in the world, although she is too modest to agree with such high praise. More importantly — at least to her — Mia helped make her team, the U.S. Women's Soccer Team, one of the best in the world. Mia helped the team win the biggest titles in the sport: the Olympic gold medal in 1996 and the World Cup in 1991 and 1999.

A MIA MOMENT

Birth Date	March 17, 1972
Height	5 feet 5 inches
Weight	125 lbs.
Home	Chapel Hill, North Carolina
Favorite Sports to Play (other than soccer)	Golf, basketball
Favorite Sport to Watch (other than soccer)	College basketball
Favorite Athletes	Hockey player Wayne Gretzky, cyclist Greg LeMond, and heptathlete and long jumper Jackie Joyner-Kersee
Favorite Food	Italian
Favorite Album	"The Joshua Tree" by U2
Superstition	Always ties her right shoelace first before a game
Secret Desire	To play on the women's pro golf tour

All this has made Mia famous, but she doesn't like attention. She hates talking to the news media. She can't avoid it, though, especially after all the hoopla over the big 1999 World Cup win. Mia is a star, whether she likes it or not. And so she has turned the burden of being famous into an opportunity to be a role model for kids and an ambassador for women's soccer. She reaches out to young girls, in particular.

"We want to get girls out to the games to see how hard we play and how fast we play. We want them to see the chemistry and intensity," Mia said. "It's another choice for them. They can say, 'I want to be a nurse.' 'I want to be a doctor.' 'I want to be a professional soccer player.'"

Being the kind of professional soccer player that Mia is would be a worthy goal for any young person, male or female. Mia always puts her team first while giving everything she's got as an individual player. She never grandstands or grabs the glory. She just plays lots of great soccer, and then shares the credit with her team-mates. Mia is an excellent example to anyone who wants to be a great athlete — or a great person.

BORROWED FROM A BALLERINA

Mia was born in Selma, Alabama, on March 17, 1972, St. Patrick's Day. She is the fourth of Stephanie and Bill Hamm's six children. Her real name is Mariel Margaret Hamm, but early on she became known as Mia. The nickname was borrowed from a ballerina who had taught her mother. Mrs. Hamm loved ballet. When Mia was five years old, Mrs. Hamm wanted her to take ballet lessons. But Mia resisted. She wanted to play soccer, instead.

Mia's brother Garrett was about three years older than she. Garrett was an orphan who was part American and part Thai (the people from Thailand, a country in southeast Asia). He had been adopted by the Hamms when he was eight. Mia adored Garrett and copied everything he did. One of Garrett's favorite activities was soccer. He was good at it, too. This helped attract Mia to the game.

The neighborhood kids played soccer and other sports. Mia tried to join in. "When they would play pickup football and start choosing teams, nobody wanted Mia because she was too little," Mrs. Hamm recalled. "But Garrett knew she had a great ability to catch the ball and hold it and run with it." Her brother's belief in Mia's athletic abilities helped give her the courage to play with other kids.

When she was five years old, Mia joined a peewee soccer team. Her talent soon was obvious: She began to score goals. For the next 10 years, she played soccer with the boys. She was usually the only girl. But she loved the sport too much to mind. And she was so good that the boys — at least those on her team — didn't mind.

Mia was a shy child, except at home. With so many kids in the family, Mia couldn't be too quiet there. Sometimes she felt shouting was the only way to be heard. "I was never very good at expressing myself. I was this really emotional kid — still am — and I would get attention by screaming and yelling," she recalled. "When I would get frustrated or upset, I didn't know how to step out of it and say 'Okay, Mia, let's think about what you say before you say it.' I was always the one apologizing later."

But Mia had nothing to apologize for on the soccer field. When Mia was 14 and living in Texas, a local coach asked his friend Anson Dorrance to come and check out this amazing young soccer player. Mr. Dorrance coached the University of North Carolina women's soccer team and the U.S. national team. He had seen good soccer players. But the first time he saw Mia was something else.

"I saw this young kid accelerate like she was shot out of a cannon," Coach Dorrance said. "Without seeing her touch the ball, I ran around saying 'Is that Mia Hamm?'"

It was Mia Hamm, all right. At 15, she joined the national team — as its youngest member ever! Coaches were impressed with her raw talent and speed. Still, Mia's move to top–flight competition was hard. "Tactically, I didn't know what to do," Mia said. "During fitness sessions, I was dying [because they were so hard]. I would cry half the time."

But Mia stuck it out. She learned and improved, but it took some time. She didn't score a goal until her 17th international match, in 1990.

After high school graduation, Mia followed Coach Dorrance to the University of North Carolina (UNC), in the town of Chapel Hill. She soon became one of the best college players in the country. UNC won the national championship each season Mia played for the team — four straight years.

She set the national record for goals scored in a career, with 103. She won the award as the best female college soccer player in the country twice.

During her college years, Mia also played on the national team that won the very first women's World Cup, in 1991. The United States beat China, 2–1, on goals by Michelle Akers.

Mia graduated in 1994 with her political–science degree. But politics wasn't on her mind. Two other subjects were — marriage and soccer. She was married in 1994 to college classmate Christian Corey. Christian became a Marine Corps helicopter pilot. Mia trained hard to improve her soccer game.

Women's soccer had never been a medal sport in the Olympics. When it was announced that it would be a medal sport at the 1996 Summer Games, in Atlanta, Georgia, Mia and her teammates were stoked! They set their sights on one goal — an Olympic gold medal. The members of the team spent a lot of time together, training hard. They also trained hard on their own. "It is an awesome group of women committed to winning, growing soccer in America, and setting a good example for young athletes every–where," Mia said.

The intense efforts by Mia and her teammates paid off. After playing five games, the United States faced China in the final. The stadium was filled with 76,481 screaming, cheering fans. The pressure was on. No problem. Mia and her fellow Americans delivered, against the tough Chinese team. Just as they had in the World Cup in 1991, the U.S. women's soccer team defeated the team from China, 2–1. The U.S. women had their gold medals.

SO, *THAT'S* HOW IT FEELS!

Mia usually plays forward — up front, where she can torment the other team's goalie. But once, Mia played way back at the other end of the field and got a taste of what it's like facing scorers like herself. She filled in as goalie for the U.S. national team!

During a 1991 World Cup match against Denmark, goalkeeper Briana Scurry was ejected for a foul. The United States had already used all its substitutions, so it could not put in another goalie. Mia was picked to step in for Briana for a few minutes. "I was scared to death," Mia remembered. "I hope I don't have to do it again." Despite her fears, Mia made one save, and the United States ended up winning the game.

Mia was a hot property. Requests for interviews flooded in. Product-endorsement offers piled up. But Mia still didn't enjoy the attention. Gradually, she got used to it as she gave more interviews and appeared on television. She also was featured in advertisements. She wrote a fitness column for *USA Weekend* magazine. She even had her own signature sneaker, the Nike Air Zoom M9. (Mia wears number 9 on her jersey.) Mia got Nike to stamp her brother Garrett's initials, GJH, on the sole of each pair.

Mia had won individual and team awards. She was the first player — male or female — ever named U.S. Soccer Athlete of the Year three times. (She won the award from 1994–96.) On May 22nd, 1999, when she scored her 108th goal, Mia became the highest scoring player in international soccer history.

But the 1999 World Cup was coming up. It would be a big tournament for the U.S. Team, in some ways bigger than any World Cup before. That's because the finals would take place in the United States. The noisy home crowd would be rooting for a second world championship. The United States had lost in the semi–finals of the previous World Cup, in 1995, to Norway. The U.S. women really wanted the Cup back. Mia's performance during the 1999 World Cup wasn't up to her usual standards. She scored twice in the first two games, and then had a long streak without a goal through the team's next three games. Mia began to doubt herself, to wonder why she wasn't scoring. But she concentrated on being the great team player she had always been, and she remained the key to the U.S. attack.

The final game of the 1999 Women's World Cup was amazing! It was played in the Rose Bowl, in California. More than 90,000 people crowded into the famous old stadium, setting a new world attendance record for a women's sports event. Forty million more tuned in to watch on television.

Just as they had at the 1996 Olympics, China and the United States faced off for the championship. The two teams fought back and forth, but no one scored during regular play. No one scored during overtime either! That meant there would be a penalty–kick shoot–out to decide the gold medal.

In a shoot–out, five players from each team take turns going one–on–one against the goalie. The goalie must stand on the goal line without moving her feet until the ball is kicked. After every player had a turn, the team with the highest number of goals wins.

The situation was tense as one player after another stepped up to the ball. The score was tied at two goals each when China's midfielder, Liu Ying, faced off against U.S. goalkeeper Briana Scurry. Ying hammered the ball, but Briana dove to her left to make an amazing save. The crowd went wild. The save gave the U.S. women the chance they needed. Unless they missed a shot, they would win.

Each team scored again, to make it 3–3. Mia was up next. The pressure was terrible. Mia, who had been struggling, didn't want to blow her team's chance for a gold medal. So she suggested that another player take her place in the shoot-out, but it was too late. She had to take the kick.

Mia walked on to the field, knowing she had to find her missing confidence. If she made her shot, it would put the United States ahead going into the final round of penalty kicks. Mia concentrated, stepped swiftly into the ball, and blasted her shot. It was perfect: Another goal for the United States! Mia had come through when it really counted.

China scored again after Mia's kick. With the scored tied 4–4, Brandi Chastain of the United States nailed one past goalie Gao Hong of China. The United States had won the shoot-out, 5–4, and won the World Cup title.

Mia ended 1999 as the world's all-time leading scorer with 114 goals and 93 career assists for 321 points.

What's even more amazing is that because of her high number of assists, if Mia had never scored a goal, she would still be in the top 10 scorers in U.S. history!

HELLO, SYDNEY

Fourteen months after the U.S. Women's Team's stunning victory at the World Cup, the team was in Sydney, Australia for the 2000 Olympics, going for the gold medal. Naturally, Mia was the "go-to" player on the team.

But the 2000 women's team was much different than the 1999 squad. A new coach, April Heinrichs, had brought in a new system and switched around some personnel. Michelle Akers had retired. The 2000 team spent seven tough months preparing for the Olympics, playing 30 games, with five tournaments. The team was tired, but ready for Olympic action.

Mia helped her team get to the gold medal game by kicking a game-winning goal against Brazil. But in the gold medal game, the U.S. team came up on the short end and lost a heartbreaking 3–2 sudden-death overtime match to Norway. The U.S. team had to settle for a silver medal.

The loss was very emotional for Mia. Holding back her tears hours after the game, she said, "There is no better feeling than putting on a U.S.A. jersey. It has been an honor. We played our hearts out, and that in a nutshell is what our team is about."

LOOKIN' GOOD

People magazine once named Mia one of the 50 most beautiful people in the world. Mia disagreed. "It's obvious that I'm not," she said. Many people think the magazine got it right, though. Said her teammate, Julie Foudy: "Mia has natural beauty. It's not something she has to spend a thousand dollars on."

Advertisers think Mia has something special that can help sell their products. Her face has turned up in many ads, for everything from Gatorade to Barbie dolls.

One thing is for sure: She looks great dashing downfield with a soccer ball on her foot and the opponent's goal in her eyes!

MAKING HISTORY

In 2001, the professional Women's United Soccer Association (WUSA) played its first season. Mia, playing for the Washington Freedom, was one of the new league's biggest stars. Some of her fellow teammates from the U.S. Women's Soccer Team joined the WUSA, too. For the first time, Mia would be playing against her former teammates, such as Brandi Chastain. "It's going to be strange," Mia said.

Mia knew that her stardom was going to put a lot of pressure on her. Many people thought that she would be largely responsible for the success of the new league. Mia didn't think so. "I look at it as a great opportunity. We've [the U.S. Women's team] been spread out and we need to be the vanguards in this effort. I want to see this league succeed," she said.

Mia set the pace for the Freedom, leading the team with six goals and 16 points over the 19-game season. Once again, Mia showed why she was the model for women's soccer in the United States for more than 10 years.

Inspired by her brother Garrett, Mia continues to shred defenses and terrify goalies. She may be shy about publicity and modest about her talent. But she is something else too, something all true athletes want to become: Mia Hamm is the very best in her sport.

>> KEN GRIFFEY, JR.

Dazzling fielding and slugging make the Cincinnati Kid a hit

They call him Junior or, sometimes, just the Kid. Either nickname fits this grown-up baseball player, even now, as he gets ready to bat in one of the most famous arenas in the world.

Ken Griffey, Jr. digs into the batter's box at Yankee Stadium, in New York City. He grinds his high-top cleats into the dirt and stares at the pitcher without blinking. It's May 8, 1999, and, as usual, sportswriters and photographers in the stadium are watching carefully. The fans and players pay attention too. They know that at any time, Junior may do something special. This is a player on his way to the Baseball Hall of Fame. No one wants to miss a feat that may take him a step closer.

Junior doesn't appear worried about the attention. The slugger rarely looks worried when he's on a baseball field. Smiles, laughter, and fun are more his style. Why, just before he walked to home plate, he was kneeling in the on-deck circle, just looking around the stands. He wasn't studying the pitcher. He was checking out the

fans behind his team's dugout. Junior could have been a Little Leaguer preparing for routine batting practice rather than a major league star.

Now, Junior stands at the plate in his Seattle Mariners uniform and waits quietly for the pitch, his face relaxed. His powerful hands and arms wave the bat around in tight circles, poised for action. New York Yankee pitcher Jay Tessmer stares in at catcher Jorge Posada for the sign.

Jay slices his first pitch across the inside corner of the plate. Junior watches it sail by. Strike one. Jay has faced Junior twice before in his career — and both times he got this slugger out. Can he do it again?

Junior doesn't let the second pitch go by. This time, he takes his trademark short stride into the ball and connects with a loud *thwack!* Junior's hands explode through the swing, propelling his black bat around and upward. The baseball soars in a beautiful arc and lands in the rightfield seats. *Home run!* It is his 361st career homer, and it ties him for 45th place on the all–time home–run list. Who is he tied with? None other than the legendary Yankee great Joe DiMaggio! Way to go, Junior.

THE BEST IN THE GAME

After the game, the reporters want to know what Junior thinks about catching up with Joe DiMaggio. Junior says that he didn't know the home run meant anything special until after he hit it. "I was sitting in the dugout when a cameraman leaned in and told me," he says, and then

GRIFFEY AT A GLANCE

Birth Date	November 21, 1969
Height	6 feet 3 inches
Weight	205 lbs.
Bats	Left
Throws	Left
Family	Melissa (wife); Trey (son), born January 19, 1994; Taryn (daughter), born October 21, 1995
Home	Orlando, Florida
Favorite Sport to Play (other than baseball)	Golf
Favorite Sport to Watch (other than baseball)	Basketball
Favorite Clothes	Jeans and sweat suits
Favorite Animal	Dogs (owns three Rottweilers)

adds: "It's nice, but it was more important we won the game, more than any homer, even one that tied me with a great player like DiMaggio."

These feelings tell you a lot about Junior. He's a ballplayer who loves the game and loves to win. He thinks about his team first. He works very hard, but enjoys himself every day at the park. He is modest about his achievements, and they are many. Junior has shown such huge talent that many people — people who understand baseball — believe he is the best in the game.

"When you look at what Junior has done and the skills he possesses, you have to say that in this era, he is as good as anyone who has played," says Lou Piniella, manager of the Seattle Mariners. "I can't think of any player in the past thirty years to compare with Junior."

A CHIP OFF THE OLD BLOCK

You could go back almost three decades to see where Junior's baseball skills started. His father, Ken Griffey, Sr. was a fine major league ballplayer in the 1970s and 1980s (*see box on page 84*). That meant that Junior — who was born in 1969 — grew up around the best baseball in the world. He had a great coach nearby: his dad.

"He had shortcuts — like my teaching him how to hit, how to turn on the ball, how to stay out of slumps," Ken, Sr. once told *Sports Illustrated*. "When [Junior] started coming of age and doing things he shouldn't . . . he'd get sent to me. I'd give him a good talking–to, then take him under the stands at Yankee Stadium, and throw him batting practice. That's where he really learned to play the game."

Ken, Sr. grew up in Donora, Pennsylvania, as one of six children in a poor family. His father left the family when Ken was just two years old. Ken was athletic. He worked hard at baseball, and at supporting his family, even as a kid.

Although he played several sports well, Ken, Sr. decided to concentrate on baseball. He turned pro after high school and spent almost five years in the minor leagues before getting a chance to play with the Cincinnati Reds in 1973. He became a key member of the Reds teams that won the World Series in 1975 and 1976.

As an important player on a successful ball club, Ken, earned good money. As a result, Ken, Jr. had no money problems, a very different experience than his dad had known. Junior sometimes rode in a Rolls Royce to Little League games. His first car was a $30,000 BMW.

Junior's mother was also athletic. Alberta "Birdie" Griffey played basketball and volleyball. She had six brothers and sisters. Her father worked at a steel mill. Birdie married Ken, Sr. right out of high school, before he was even playing pro baseball. They lived through some tough years with little money before Ken, Sr. hit the big time.

George Kenneth Griffey, Jr., their first child, was born in Donora on November 21, 1969. Ken, Sr. had just finished his rookie season in the minors. He was only 19 years old — the very age Junior would be when he broke into the major leagues. Later, Junior was joined by a brother, Craig, and then a sister, Lathesia.

By the time Junior was three, he was playing Wiffle ball, and later he starred in the Reds' annual father–son baseball games. When he started playing organized baseball, Junior dominated. In Little League, he threw so hard that opposing hitters sometimes cried because they were afraid of being hit by his pitches. When he was 16, Junior competed against 18–year-olds in Connie Mack League Baseball. He smashed three homers in the league's 1986 World Series.

Junior didn't start playing for his school team until his junior year in high school. He became a star anyway. He set several records and attracted many major league scouts at Archbishop Moeller High, in Cincinnati, Ohio. On June 2, 1987, the Seattle Mariners made Junior the first person chosen in that year's major league draft of amateur players. They gave him a $160,000 bonus when he signed a contract with them. Junior was only 17.

Junior started out at the lowest level of minor league ball, Rookie League. He had never lived away from home. He was in for a big shock during his first year in the minors.

Junior played in Bellingham, Washington, about 90 miles north of Seattle. His team rode to the games on a 30–year-old bus. Some trips took 10 hours. But it wasn't just the length of the trip. Junior told reporters that one of the bus driver's sons called him racist names and another son threatened to gun him down. "I didn't know what to do," Junior recalled. "All I knew is I wanted to go home."

The problems affected Junior's play. He performed poorly, and he didn't hustle on the field. It looked as if he didn't want to be there. But his mother came to see him to find out what was wrong. She sternly urged him to tough it out and concentrate on his career. He did, and ended the season with strong numbers: a .313 batting average, 14 homers, and 43 runs batted in. *Baseball America* magazine named Junior the top prospect in the minors.

Junior was still struggling with his feelings, though. When he returned home after his rookie year, he began to have arguments with his father. Ken, Sr. expected Junior to be responsible and move to his own apartment or pay rent to his parents. "I was confused," Junior later told the *Seattle Times*. "I was hurting, and I wanted to cause some hurt for others."

Junior was so unhappy and confused that he did a terrible thing. In January 1988, he tried to commit suicide by swallowing 277 aspirin pills. He threw up. His girlfriend's mother raced him to the hospital and afterward, he was fine.

Junior doesn't discuss his attempt to kill himself any more. After all, it happened a long time ago, when he was still a teenager. But he did speak to a reporter about it once because he wanted others to learn from him that suicide is never the right solution to troubles in your life.

Junior and his father began to have long talks after this. They settled many of the problems between them. As Junior settled down emotionally, his game improved. In the 1988 season, Junior moved on with his career in a big way. He performed well and swiftly rose through the minor leagues, playing for teams in California and Vermont.

Junior was invited to the Mariner training camp, before the 1989 season. There, he continued to come on strong. He set a Mariner spring training record by getting at least one hit in 15 straight games. He also swatted his way to team records for hits and RBIs, batting an impressive .359 in the exhibition season. And he played brilliantly on defense.

THE SENIOR GRIFFEY

Ken, Sr. was not a superstar, as his son has become. But he was one of the fastest runners and most dependable hitters on one of the greatest teams in baseball history. From 1973 through 1981, Ken hit .311 and stole 150 bases for the Cincinnati Reds. In 1976, when he hit .336, he almost won the National League batting title. Together with talented teammates such as Pete Rose, Johnny Bench, Joe Morgan, and others, he led the "Big Red Machine" to World Series wins in 1975 and 1976.

Ken later played for the New York Yankees, the Atlanta Braves, and the Reds again (from 1988 to 1990). Then, on August 29, 1990, he was signed by the Mariners. Senior and Junior became the first father-son combo to play for the same major league team at the same time. Ken, Sr. retired after the 1991 season. He finished with a .296 career batting average, 200 stolen bases, and 2,143 hits over 19 seasons.

Still, the coaches weren't sure this kid was ready for the pressure of daily big–league play. He had only been through two years in the minors, after all. And he was just 19. But Junior felt sure. He knew there was still much to learn, but he also felt confident about tackling the major leagues. Finally, then–Manager Jim Lefebvre *[le-FEE-ver]* announced his decision to this budding baseball star: "Congratulations! You're my starting centerfielder," he told Junior in March.

Junior was delighted. And so was his dad, because this news fulfilled a dream for both Ken Griffeys. They would become the first father and son to play in the major leagues at the same time.

April 3, 1989, was the historic day. Ken, Sr. played for the Cincinnati Reds, against the Los Angeles Dodgers. Junior played for the Mariners, against the Oakland A's. Dad did not get a hit that day. Junior did. In his first official major league at-bat, he smacked a double off Oakland ace Dave Stewart. It was just the beginning.

A RECORD BREAKER

During his first 13 seasons in the majors, Junior set more records and earned more important honors than anyone expected. Even Junior himself couldn't have anticipated so much success so fast. Let the numbers from his first 13 seasons (through 2001) tell the story:

- In 1997 and 1998, Junior hammered 56 home runs. No, not 56 total — 56 in each season. That was after hitting 49 in 1996. In 1999, he hit 48.
- He hit 460 career homers and, at age 31, was just shy of reaching the 500-homer milestone.

And he has done all this despite missing 51 games in the 1994 season due to the baseball strike, and another 163 games due to injuries in 1995, 1996, and 2001.

The statistics go on and on:
- Junior batted over .300 six times between 1989 and 1999.
- In 1998, Junior became just the third player to have more than 140 RBIs three seasons in a row. The other ballplayers who accomplished this feat were Babe Ruth and Lou Gehrig — pretty good company.
- Junior also stole 20 bases for the first time in 1998, and then stole 24 in 1999.

Junior is an outstanding defensive player as well. Through 2001, he had won ten Gold Glove awards in a row for fielding excellence.

But Junior had done amazing things before. In 1997, he helped the Mariners win a then-team-record 90 games. He led the A.L. with 56 home runs and 147 RBIs. So that year, sportswriters named him the A.L.'s Most Valuable Player.

Fans love Junior. From 1990 to 2000 Junior was voted onto 11 consecutive All-Star teams. Each time he was selected as a starter. Four of those times he was elected by wider margins than anyone in the majors. Fans find Junior exciting to watch, at bat and in the field. They feel that he makes the game fun.

Before the start of the 2000 season, Junior was traded by Seattle to the Cincinnati Reds. Junior was finally going to be playing full-time in front of his hometown fans. From the moment Junior signed with the Reds, everyone knew his arrival in Cincinnati would be front-page news. When Junior showed up at the Reds' 2000 spring training camp in Sarasota, Florida, dozens of reporters were there to cover his arrival.

JUNIOR "BATS" .500!

There are many Internet sites dedicated to Junior, but he has his own site.

In the June 8, 1999, entry of "Junior's Journal," Junior stuck his neck out with two bold sports predictions. He said that Tiger Woods would win the U.S. Open golf tournament and that the San Antonio Spurs would nab the NBA championship. Junior was right about the Spurs. They defeated the New York Knicks in the NBA Finals. But Tiger did not win the U.S. Open. (Payne Stewart did.) Half right isn't so bad, though. As a fortune teller, you could say that Junior is batting .500.

Junior's first season in Cincinnati had its shares of highs and lows. Throughout the season, he was bothered by knee and hamstring injuries. Although Junior was voted to the All-Star Game lineup, he didn't play in the game because of a knee injury.

On September 11, Junior tore his left hamstring when he crashed into Chicago Cubs' catcher Joe Girardi while trying to score. Junior had to be helped from the field. At first, it was thought that Junior would be out of action for only a few days. Unfortunately, the injury was more serious than doctors thought. Junior did not start another game for the rest of the season. After the injury, Junior made only three pinch–hitting appearances, hitting his 40th home run in one of them.

Despite the injury, Junior lit up the 2000 season with plenty of fireworks. In the 145 games he played, Junior led the Reds in homers (40), RBIs (118), runs scored (100), total bases (289), and walks (94). He knocked in 100 RBIs for the fifth straight season, and eighth time in his career.

Junior's home runs paid off handsomely for the Reds. The team had a record of 24–11 when he homered, and 18 of his 40 dingers either tied games, or put the Reds ahead. However, the Reds dropped to an 85–77 record, winning 11 fewer games than they did in 1999. They finished second in the National League Central Division. Junior's first year with Cincinnati had been one to remember. Little did he know that more disappointment was on its way.

The 2001 season spelled T–R–O–U–B–L–E for Junior and the Reds even before the season started. In a spring training game against the Kansas City Royals, Ken strained his left hamstring while rounding third base as he was heading home. Junior pulled up sharply, fell on his back, and grabbed his leg in pain. The same bad hamstring that had knocked him out of action last September was injured once again.

The team decided to keep Junior out of the starting lineup indefinitely, rather than place him on the disabled list. Junior doesn't like missing games and believed he could still contribute to the team even with his painful hamstring injury. He was given pinch-hitting chores early in 2001.

In late April, Junior aggravated his hamstring in a pinch-hitting appearance against the Colorado Rockies while running out of the batter's box. That was it for Junior. He was placed on the disabled list for the first time since 1995, on April 29. "Why take a chance at this point? We tried something [using Junior as a pinch hitter], it didn't work," said team medical director Dr. Timothy Kremchek. Junior's stats up to that time read 0-for-12 with three walks as a pinch hitter.

Junior sat out the next six weeks, giving the injury time to heal while exercising to strengthen the hamstring. But Junior finally did get back on the field on June 16, going 1-for-3 with a single against the Rockies. Cincinnati coach Bob Boone knew it was going to take a while for Junior to feel totally comfortable once again. "It's spring training time for him . . . When he realizes that he can run and the leg won't fall off, he'll be more natural and just play," said Bob.

Junior cracked his first home run of the 2001 season on June 19 against the Milwaukee Brewers. (Junior's last home run had been on September 19, 2000.) In his first five games back, Junior was 7-for-18, with one homer and five RBIs.

Junior found his groove in August when he put everyone on notice that the Master Blaster was back. Against the San Francisco Giants on August 9, Junior became the youngest player to reach 450 career home runs when he crushed a Russ Ortiz pitch over the right field wall in Cincinnati. Junior was 31 years 261 days old when he hit the historic blast — 15 days younger than Jimmie Foxx, who held the record previously. Junior was unstoppable in August, pounding 11 homers with 29 RBIs.

On the season, Junior played in only 111 games, but managed to put up very respectable numbers. He led the Reds in homers with 22, and his .286 batting average was his personal best since 1997. The Reds sank to a 66–96 record while Junior's former team, the Mariners, were on their way to setting the American League record for most wins in a season with 116.

STILL HAVING FUN

Junior's good nature and positive attitude are one big reason that Junior has held on to the kid in himself. The multi–millionaire slugger still calls his father *collect* to make him pay the bill. He plays video games and listens to rap music. He still brings his joy in playing baseball to the ballpark. During warm–ups, he often wears his cap back-ward. He kids his teammates. Most days, Junior wears a broad grin as he strides across the field.

"When I was growing up, my dad always told me, 'Have fun,'" Junior said. "'Don't worry if you make an out. Just do the best job you can.'"

And that is what Junior does, month after month, year after year — even when times are tough for him or for his team. His "best job" has been outstanding. The ability to be outstanding day in and day out have made Junior a true star.

>> ALEX RODRIGUEZ

He's become baseball's best player with style, grace — and a movie-star's handsome face

Shortstop Alex Rodriguez had it all going his way. At 17, he was the Number 1 pick in the baseball draft. At 18, he was in the major leagues. By the age of 20, he was on his way to becoming a superstar. Not only was he an All-Star by age 21, but — like Derek Jeter of the New York Yankees — "A-Rod" had become a fan heartthrob. Girls loved his movie-star good looks, and everybody who followed baseball admired his talent and success.

Then it happened.

Alex, then with Seattle Mariners, was doing agility exercises in spring training just days before the beginning of the 1999 season. He jumped over a box, fell, and tore a ligament in his left knee. He needed surgery and missed the next five weeks of the season. It was the first major mishap of Alex's career and the first time he had ever had surgery. He was stunned. "I never thought it would happen to me," said Alex.

It had happened, so the question became: Would Alex be able to play at his usual high level when he returned to the diamond? Some people, including Alex, were not sure.

But two of his teammates at the time — outfielder Jay Buhner and designated hitter Edgar Martinez — reassured Alex that he would be okay. They had gone through surgery themselves and come back. Fans also wrote to Alex, telling him to keep his chin up.

"I got so many letters from doctors and lawyers and people who said they had had the same surgery and that I would be back in no time," says Alex. "That was very encouraging."

AS GOOD AS NEW

Alex worked out hard to get back into shape. When he returned to the Mariners in the middle of May, he began to play like his old super self. He blasted a monstrous 437-foot homer against the San Diego Padres in an inter-league in June. By the All-Star Game in July, he had hit two homers in one game four times. A-Rod was A-okay.

Alex had faced his toughest challenge and come out on top. "It's very hard to come back after you're injured," he says. "But I had to keep believing in myself. I kept telling myself I'd be as good as new."

He had that right. Alex finished the 1999 season with 42 home runs, which tied for fifth in the American League — despite having missed those five weeks. He also had 111 RBIs and a .285 batting average. He stole 21 bases and would have stolen more if he hadn't been worried about hurting his knee again.

It turned out to be another amazing season from an amazing player. Alex is so good that some fans think he's the best player in baseball. And Alex is young: he turned only 27 years old in 2002.

"I can't wait 'till I hit my prime," says Alex.

AWESOME POWER

Alex can do just about everything on a baseball field, but the thing that sets him apart from other shortstops is his awesome power at the plate. Traditionally, teams expect shortstops to just be good fielders and to maybe run the bases well. But Alex can go deep, like the best sluggers in the game.

"I've watched A-Rod hit homers to leftfield, centerfield, and rightfield," says Sean Casey, the first baseman for the Cincinnati Reds. "He makes it look so easy."

Alex mashed 148 taters during his first four–plus seasons in the majors. That's far more home runs than any shortstop under age 25 had ever hit in the history of baseball. In fact, when Alex hit 42 homers in 1998, it was the most ever in one season by an American League shortstop. He tied his own home run record in 1999. In 2001, he set the major league record for most homers by a shortstop with 52.

Shortstop Omar Vizquel of the Cleveland Indians thinks Alex could hit homers like single-season record holder Barry Bonds if that's what Alex wanted to do. "I think Alex has a chance to break the [single-season] home-run record," says Omar.

AWESOME ALL-AROUND

Alex can do more than hit homers. He stole 46 bases along with his 42 home runs in 1998 to become just the third member of the "40–40" club (players who hit 40 or more homers and steal 40 or more bases in one season). Barry Bonds of the San Francisco Giants and Jose Canseco of the Chicago White Sox are the other two.

Alex also hits for a high average and plays sharp defense. Good as he is, he is always striving to improve.

"I have such a long way to go," says Alex. "Unless you hit one thousand and make no errors, you can always improve in this game."

Other players think Alex is awfully good already.

"He's the best ballplayer in the game," first baseman David Segui of the Baltimore Orioles told the *Seattle Post-Intelligencer* newspaper. "Definitely, Barry Bonds and Ken Griffey, Jr. are up there with him, but the way Alex plays the game sets him apart from everyone else. He plays the game with great intensity, the way it's supposed to be played — to win. The way he goes about it day in and day out, with a desire to get better . . . it's very impressive."

Even Derek Jeter, the New York Yankees' star shortstop, is an A-Rod fan. Says Derek: "He's one of the fastest players in the league. I told him he should go for 50–50."

Alexander Emmanuel Rodriguez was born on July 27, 1975, in New York City. He has an older brother, Joe, and a sister, Susy. His parents are from the Dominican Republic, a small island nation in the Caribbean Sea. The family moved back to the Dominican Republic when Alex was four years old. Victor Rodriguez, Alex's father, was a catcher in a Dominican professional league. He introduced Alex to baseball.

After four years in the Dominican Republic, the family moved to Kendall, Florida, near Miami. But Alex's father left the family when Alex was 10. Alex kept hoping his dad would return, but he never did. "It was hard," says Alex. "I did my best to help out around the house and bring home good grades to make my mom proud."

MAMA'S PRIDE

Alex's mom, Lourdes, worked as a secretary during the day and nights as a waitress to help support Alex, Joe, and Susy. "When mom got home, I'd always count her tip money to see how good she did," said Alex. "She taught me the meaning of hard work and commitment."

Alex repaid his mom by making her proud in many ways. He became an honor student at Westminster Christian School and the best high school baseball player in the United States. (Alex also played quarterback on the high school football team and point guard on the basketball team.) Alex was lucky to have Westminster baseball coach Rich Hofman as a mentor and friend. He spent hours in Coach Hofman's office talking about school, life, and sports. Coach Hofman encouraged Alex to work hard. In his first season on the team, Alex batted only .280.

Coach Hofman taught Alex one of baseball's golden rules: Be patient and swing at good pitches. Alex also needed to beef up, so he started lifting weights. He also did 100 push-ups and 100 sit-ups each morning.

The hard work paid off. In his junior year, Alex hit a hefty .450 and Westminster won the 1992 national high school championship.

The following year, Alex batted a monstrous .505 and swiped 35 bases in 35 attempts. But everything did not go right: Alex made a crucial throwing error that helped cost his team a chance to win the national championship again. Alex cried on the bench after the game. "That was real hard to come back from," he says. "But I had to put it behind me . . . It's always in my mind. That's why I don't take anything for granted."

The Seattle Mariners made it easier for Alex to move on. They had the first pick in baseball's 1993 amateur draft and could have picked any high school or college player in the country. The Mariners chose Alex. Alex signed with the Mariners for $1.3 million over three years. Alex treated himself royally by buying a $30,000 Cherokee Jeep.

After playing in only 82 minor league games, Alex was called up to Seattle in July 1994. At age 18, he was the youngest starting shortstop in the majors since 1974, when Hall of Famer Robin Yount started for the Milwaukee Brewers. But when Alex hit only .204 in 17 games, the Mariners decided that he wasn't quite ready for prime time.

Alex thought he would be the Mariners' starting shortstop in 1995, but he was called up and sent back down to the minors three times during the 1995 season. Seattle was in a tight pennant race and they didn't think that their 19-year-old shortstop could handle the pressure. They shifted him back and forth between Seattle and the minor leagues all season in 1995.

Alex got so discouraged that he wanted to go home and play baseball at the University of Miami. His mom told him to keep trying.

Alex did.

ONE-MAN WRECKING CREW

It wasn't until spring training of 1996 that Alex, who was still only 20 years old, became the Mariners' starting shortstop for good. He was a one-man wrecking crew that season. He led the majors with a .358 batting average and blasted 36 home runs. He also led the league in doubles (54), grand slams (3), total bases (379), and runs scored (141). Alex also rapped out 215 hits, the most ever by a shortstop in one season.

Alex missed being named the A.L. MVP by one vote. Outfielder Juan Gonzalez of the Texas Rangers won the honor. It was the closest MVP vote in 36 years.

"I think it was a surprise for everyone," Alex says about his breakout season. "It certainly was a pleasant surprise for me."

BIG-LEAGUE IDOL

As a kid, Alex kept a life-sized poster of Cal Ripken, Jr. on the wall above his bed. In Little League, Alex imitated the way Cal flipped throws to first base. Alex is now a tall, powerful hitter and graceful fielder, like Cal was during his 21 years with the Baltimore Orioles. Alex is a lot like Cal in another way, too. Cal always treated the fans with respect. "Now that I'm a big leaguer, I try to show the same respect," says Alex.

Alex's numbers slipped to 23 homers with 84 RBIs and a .300 batting average in 1997. He was selected to the A.L. All-Star team for the second year in a row and there was little doubt around the league that he would be one of the premier players for years to come. His selection as the starting shortstop in the All-Star Game broke Cal Ripken, Jr.'s streak of 13 straight starts at the position. Alex was at the head of a youth movement sweeping through major league baseball.

Alex says that watching Ken Griffey, Jr. play every day helped him succeed quickly in the majors. The two team-mates became friends who played video games together. "Ken teaches you that you can have fun, respect the game, and also play it hard," says Alex. "When you have that combination, you're going to put yourself in a position to be successful."

Says Junior: "Alex works hard. He's a smart kid. Everyone knows he's going to be a special player."

UPS AND DOWNS

Alex showed everyone just how special he was in 2000. He opened the season on a tear, batting .405 in his first 12 games. By mid-season, he was batting .345 with 24 homers and 78 RBIs. Alex was selected for the 2000 All-Star team, but a pair of injuries kept him from playing in the game.

On July 7, he was knocked unconscious in a collision with Los Angeles Dodger shortstop Alex Cora in an inter league game. He collided with Cora in a play at second base while trying to break up a double play. Alex sustained a concussion and a strained right knee that not only prevented him from playing in the All-Star Game, but forced him to miss 13 games.

Once back in the lineup, Alex didn't waste any time picking up where he left off. In his first 15 games back in action, he batted at a .377 clip. On the year, Alex posted some of the best numbers of his career, batting .316 with 41 homers and 132 RBIs, a career high. He also drew 100 walks, by far the best in his career.

Alex's performance helped the Mariners get to the 2000 playoffs. The Mariners won the American League wild card spot and swept the Chicago White Sox in their division championship series. The Mariners then took on the defending world champion New York Yankees. The Yanks beat Seattle in the ALCS, four games to two.

Alex batted .409 with two homers and five RBIs in the six-game loss to the Yankees, giving him an overall batting average of .371 in both playoff series. The Mariners had provided the Yankees with their toughest playoff challenge even though New York went on to win the World Series. With Alex as the backbone of the club, Seattle had established itself as a powerhouse team of the future.

IN GOOD COMPANY

While establishing himself as one of the elite players in the majors, Alex became friends with such elite players as Derek Jeter and now-retired Baltimore Oriole great Cal Ripken, Jr. Alex was invited to play one-on-one basketball against Cal a few years ago in the gym at Cal's house. Each player won one game. Says Cal: "He dunked a few times, but not on me. I fouled him before I let him dunk on me!"

Alex and Derek are best pals. When Alex would visit New York to play the Yankees, he would often stay at Derek's apartment. When the Yankees played in Seattle, Derek stayed with Alex. Says Derek: "We enjoy competing against each other. When he hits a homer, he sits on the bench and flexes his arms at me."

HOME ON THE RANGE

At the end of the 2000 season, Alex's contract with the Mariners was up. He became a free agent who could negotiate a new deal with any team he chose. Clubs were lining up to sign him, including the Mariners.

The New York Mets were interested. So were the Colorado Rockies and the Texas Rangers. Whoever signed Alex would have to pay handsomely for his all-star services.

As the weeks during the off-season passed, baseball fans closely followed the story of where Alex would play in 2001. Finally, the Texas Rangers won the bidding war and signed Alex to a $252 million, 10-year deal. Alex was now the highest paid baseball player in history. Mariners' fans were plenty disappointed — and many were angry — that Alex had left the team to earn more money somewhere else.

Expectations for Alex were astronomical. The Rangers had never made it past the first round of the playoffs, and all eyes were on Alex to get them over the hump. Rangers' owner Tom Hicks said, "Alex is the player we believe will allow this franchise to fulfill its dream of continuing on its path to becoming a World Series champion."

Mr. Hicks's praise didn't end there. "Our judgment is that Alex will break every record in baseball before he finishes his career," Mr. Hicks said.

While everyone was buzzing about Alex's huge contract, he tried to play down the big money. "I don't think money really changes you. You have to remember that it doesn't make you who you are. I might make a lot of money, and people make a big deal about it. I still see myself as just a baseball player," Alex said.

Even Alex's high school coach, Rich Hofman had something to say about all the attention Alex's contract was getting. "Everyone sees him as the two-hundred fifty-two million dollar man," Coach Hofman said. "But I still see him as just Alex. We talk about life, how things are going. He's still got that kid in him."

OPENING DAY JITTERS

Alex was nervous the first time he walked into the Ranger clubhouse in spring training before the start of the 2001 season. He just didn't know how his new teammates would react to his presence. "It was like the first day of school all over again," Alex said. But things went just fine. "The veterans on this team made it easier. They wanted me here. That made me feel welcome."

With the entire baseball world closely looking on, the Rangers opened the 2001 season against the Toronto Blue Jays. The day had come for Alex to make his heralded debut in a Texas uniform. In his first fielding chance of the season, he made a throwing error. On the very next play, he stumbled on a seam in the artificial turf. As if that wasn't bad enough, Alex later tripped on his loose shoelace and flopped facedown on another play. "This game has a funny way of chewing you up and spitting you out," Alex joked after the game. It wasn't all bad, though. Alex had a pair of singles, including the season's first major league hit.

"You have to start somewhere. There was a little bit of everything: an error, a slip, hits. But it's only one game. There's one-hundred-sixty-one more. You just move on," Alex said.

Move on is exactly what he did. Two weeks later, Alex brought his .341 batting average to Seattle's SafeCo Field. He was going to play in front of Mariners' fans for the first time in a Rangers' uniform. Every time he stepped to the plate, many Seattle fans booed loudly or chanted "Pay-Rod!" Some fans held up signs that read "A-Wad" and "A-Rod, Please Buy Me a House." They threw fake money from the upper decks and booed him as loudly as they once cheered him.

Alex didn't let the razzing upset him. "I think it's all in fun. That's why they're some of the greatest fans. They were in post season form. If I was wearing a Mariners' uniform tonight, they would have been cheering for me," he said.

MIRED IN LAST PLACE

Some Mariners' fans might have been holding a grudge toward Alex, but Rangers' fans were delighted he was in Texas. Alex was selected to the All-Star team for the fifth time and his numbers by early August ranked with some of the best of his career. Alex was batting .321 with 33 homers and 99 RBIs.

THE A-ROD BRIEF

Birth Date	July 27, 1975
Weight	210 lbs.
Home	Highland Park, Dallas, Texas
Favorite Foods	Rice and beans, salmon, pasta
Favorite Sports Thrill	Beating the Chicago White Sox in the 2000 playoffs
Person I'd Like to Spend a Day With	Leonardo DaVinci
Favorite Animal	German Shepherd
Favorite Band	The Rolling Stones
Best Birthday Present	Four-year contract with the Mariners in 1996
Favorite Hobbies	Reading and traveling
Favorite Actor	Eddie Murphy

All would have been well in Texas had it not been for the Rangers' terrible performance as a team in 2001. They finished last in their division with a 73–89 record, forty-three games behind the division-leading Seattle Mariners, Alex's former team. Alex's financial fortunes might have taken a positive swing when he signed with the Rangers, but he was now playing for a team mired in the cellar of their division.

On a personal note, Alex put together one of the top offensive seasons ever by a major league shortstop. Alex hit more than 40 homers for the fourth straight year. He led the league in homers (52), runs scored (133), total bases (393), and extra-base hits (87).

Before the start of the season with Texas, Alex said, "I have to get to know new people: a new manager, a new ballpark. This is going to be a very challenging year."

Alex certainly met the challenge. He passed the test with flying colors.

>> SAMMY SOSA

There are more than homers on the mind of this slugger

Home-run madness was in full swing. It was the summer of 1998 and the entire United States, it seemed, was fascinated by the intense, but friendly, home-run race between Mark McGwire of the St. Louis Cardinals and Sammy Sosa of the Chicago Cubs. By late September, both sluggers had passed the long-time, single-season record of 61 homers. They were in new territory, both having hit more home runs than any major league player had ever hit in one year. Only one question remained: Who would finish the season with more homers — Big Mac or Slammin' Sammy? Who would be crowned America's new Home-Run King?

Two men had held that unofficial, but very special, title for most of the 20th century. The Sultan of Swat, Babe Ruth, had been baseball's Home-Run King from 1919 until 1961. Roger Maris claimed the title in 1961, when he smacked 61 homers. What an achievement it would be for either Sammy or Mark to take over that famous title.

Sammy and Mark were both good sports during their competition. They joked on television about their rivalry and wished each other well. Still, each player wanted very much to end up as the home-run champ.

As the season drew to a close, the lead changed hands often. Mark would pound a few out of the park, and then Sammy would follow. On September 23, Sammy belted two homers to tie Mark, with 65 each. Two days later, both players ripped another one to keep the chase even at 66. This race was going right down to the wire.

Meanwhile, far from the major league ballparks, something terrible happened. A fierce hurricane battered several islands in the Caribbean. One of the islands worst hit was the Dominican Republic, Sammy's home country. Sammy grew up and learned to play baseball in the Dominican Republic. Most of his family and his wife's family lived there still. In fact, Sammy himself still lives there part of each year. Hurricane Georges had destroyed much of Sammy's home country.

Sammy could not put the hurricane victims out of his mind. Many athletes probably would have. They would have focused entirely on being in the greatest home-run race ever. Or they might have focused on the race for the pennant that their team was in. But Sammy couldn't stop worrying about the people in the Dominican Republic. Sammy knew how much suffering a natural disaster like a hurricane could cause.

On September 25, the day he hit his 66th home run, Sammy announced that he was setting up the Sammy Sosa Foundation. The Foundation would make sure to aid his stricken country. After the game on September 26, Sammy rushed to the Dominican consulate in Houston, Texas. There, Sammy, along with a couple of other players, helped load supplies and food to be shipped to his country. The home-run chase with Mark was important to Sammy. But helping people in serious trouble receive emergency water, food, and shelter was also important.

Sammy didn't hit a home run on September 26 or 27, when the Cubs played their last regular-season games. He finished the year with 66. Mark hit four in his last two games to end the year with 70 homers. Some people may wonder whether Sammy's worries about the hurricane damage cost him the chance to at least tie Mark's record. No one knows for sure, of course. But we do know that, without Sammy's attention, fewer hurricane victims would have been helped.

So Mark ended up as the homer king. But Sammy did okay, too. He batted .308 and knocked in 158 runs — more than anyone else in the majors. Sammy's great performance also helped the Chicago Cubs make it to the playoffs for the first time since 1989. For his efforts, Sammy was named the National League Most Valuable Player.

The 1998 home-run race also made Sammy famous. All the fans following the race got to see what Sammy and

THE SAMMY FILE

Birth Date   November 12, 1968

Height   6 feet

Weight   210 lbs.

Bats   Right

Throws   Right

Family   Sonia (wife), Keysha (daughter), Kenia (daughter), Sammy (son), Michael (son)

Homes   Chicago, Illinois and San Pedro de Macoris, Dominican Republic

Favorite Sport to Play (other than baseball)   Boxing

Favorite Sport to Watch (other than baseball)   Football

Favorite Athlete   Michael Jordan

Best Friend   Manny Alexander, who played with Sammy on the Cubs from 1997-99

Best Advice He Ever Received   "Do good deeds, and never hurt anyone" – from his mom

Mark were like. They both became popular across the United States. People learned that Sammy had humble beginnings and that he was grateful for all baseball had given him. They discovered and came to respect his sense of humor and good sportsmanship. And they admired his efforts to help others, before and after the hurricane.

A TOUGH BEGINNING

Long before the hurricane or the home-run race or before Sammy even started playing baseball, it looked as if Sammy didn't have much of a chance to make it big in life. He was just a poor kid from a remote island. No one ever thought he would grow up to become a baseball star.

He was born Samuel Sosa on November 12, 1968, in San Pedro de Macoris, a city in the Dominican Republic. Sammy was one of seven children raised by his mother. His father died when Sammy was just seven years old. He lived with his large family in a two-room section of what had been a public hospital. There was rarely enough food to go around. To help make money, Sammy sold oranges for 10 cents and shined shoes for a quarter on street corners. Sammy also had a speech problem. Kids called him *Gago*, a Spanish word for "stutterer." Life was hard for Sammy.

Sammy liked playing baseball. He just played for fun with poor or homemade equipment. His first glove was made from a milk carton. Rolled-up socks were his "baseballs." Most players who make it to the major leagues start learning good baseball techniques when they are very young. Because he was poor, Sammy didn't play any organized ball until he was 14. But just two years after he joined his first team, a major league scout invited Sammy to a tryout.

For the tryout, Sammy had to borrow a uniform, and his shoes had a hole in them. He was a skinny 5 feet 10 inches and 150 pounds. He wasn't a fast runner, and he had a wild swing that was too long and loopy.

Still, there were things about Sammy that the scout liked. He was aggressive in the field, and the baseball jumped off his bat. That was enough. The scout signed him to a minor league contract with the Texas Rangers' organization, and Sammy had his big break into professional baseball. The scout gave Sammy a $3,500 contract. That wasn't much by major league standards, but it was a lot more money than Sammy had ever seen.

In 1986, Sammy headed to Florida to play for the Rangers' rookie–league team. Leaving his mother crying at the airport, the teenager flew off to a strange country to start a new and very different life. Sammy didn't speak any English. At first, communicating with teammates and coaches was tough.

"I was lucky because there were some [Spanish–speaking] Puerto Rican players who I hung out with. They helped me a lot," Sammy recalled. "This is the way I was able to understand the life here in the United States."

Sammy's skills needed a lot of polishing. Still, he played well enough to keep moving up through the minor leagues. In 1989, he played in 25 major league games with the

Rangers. But Sammy was soon sent back to a Triple–A team (the highest level in the minor leagues). Then, on July 29, he was traded to the Chicago White Sox.

Sammy had mixed results with the Sox. In 1990, he was the only American Leaguer to hit 10 or more doubles, triples, homers, and stolen bases. But he also made 13 fielding errors (a lot for an outfielder), struck out 150 times, and batted only .233. In 1991, he batted .203 and hit just 10 homers. Sammy was traded again before the 1992 season began. This time he went across town to the Chicago Cubs.

The move took adjustment because Sammy had never played in the National League. (The Rangers and White Sox are both American League teams.) There were different pitchers and stadiums to get to know. Sammy still had a great deal to learn. "When he first got here [in 1992], you could see he had great physical skills," said then–Chicago first baseman Mark Grace. "But he was so raw. He didn't know how to play the game."

In 1992, Sammy appeared in only 67 games because of fractures in his right hand and left ankle. But the next season, he began to show his real potential. He banged 33 homers and drove in 93 runs in 1993. He also stole 36 bases to become the first Cub admitted into the "30–30 club." That's a tough "club" to join. You have to have enough power to hit at least 30 homers and enough speed to steal 30 or more bases in one season. It requires a special combination of skills that few players have.

Sammy became the Cubs' regular rightfielder and he posted some impressive numbers over the next four seasons. Among the highlights: He stole 34 bases in 1995, hit 40 home runs in 1996, and knocked in 119 runs in 1997. His batting average climbed as high as .300, in 1994.

But Sammy wasn't consistent. In 1997, he hit only .251. He struck out often, too. That was because he seemed to always be swinging for the fences, as if he thought every hit could be a home run. Sammy also made too many reckless attempts to steal bases. He appeared to be trying to get big statistics for himself instead of working to help his team win ball games.

But there was a reason behind Sammy's behavior. It went back to his poor childhood. It seemed that Sammy thought he needed to steal a lot of bases and hit a lot of home runs in order to keep his job. As a result, he tried too hard to hit a home run or steal a base every chance he had.

That is understandable. Even though he was a wealthy man by 1997, and owned nice houses, drove expensive cars, and gave lots of money to charity, he still had a fear of being poor. And it's not easy to change.

Still, Sammy knew he had to find some way to change his thinking if he really wanted to become a better ballplayer. So, after the 1997 season, he worked with the Cubs' hitting coach Jeff Pentland for the first time. He saw a videotape of himself that showed how rushed and wild his swing was.

During the winter, he concentrated on hitting to rightfield. He finally developed the patience and poise of a fine hitter. He had become a new man at the plate.

"There was too much pressure last year," Sammy admitted in 1998. "I was trying to hit two home runs in one at bat. Now I don't feel that [way] anymore."

The difference was soon obvious to everyone. Sammy's bat was ablaze. In June 1998, he broke the major league home run record for a single month by swatting 20 homers.

WHAT'S IN A NUMBER?

In Sammy's case, quite a lot. Sammy wears number 21 on his Cub uniform. This is in honor of Roberto Clemente, a former star outfielder for the Pittsburgh Pirates who also wore 21. Like Sammy, Roberto was an outstanding player and human being. In 1972, Roberto was delivering supplies to earthquake victims in Nicaragua. The plane Roberto was in crashed, and he died. Roberto was only 38 years old and in the middle of a great career. Roberto's legend lives on. He's a member of the Baseball Hall of Fame. Major league baseball's annual award for the player who best combines outstanding baseball skills with caring for his community is named after him. And Sammy wears his number 21 on his back.

Some people develop a big head after so much success. But if anything, Sammy seemed more modest than ever. When reporters and photographers asked Sammy if he would break Roger Maris's homer record, he just talked about Big Mac. "Mark McGwire is the man," he would say. "Maybe tomorrow he'll be motivated . . . and hit two or three [home runs]."

Sammy also seemed to enjoy himself a great deal whenever he was at the ballpark. "Every day a holiday for Sammy Sosa," he would say with a laugh. After Sammy belted a homer, he always kissed two fingers, touched his heart, and then blew a kiss. This was a message to his mom, who watched the Cub games on television in the Dominican Republic.

A GOOD SPORT

Sammy's happy style was contagious. It helped make the great home-run race of 1998 a special pleasure to watch. Sammy kept the smile on his face even on the day that Big Mac broke Roger Maris's homer record first. As it happened, Sammy was right there when Mark hit that historic homer. Everyone could see how he handled it — perfectly. Right after Mark's homer, Sammy trotted in from rightfield and warmly hugged his rival.

"It was a great moment," Sammy said later. "I could see the emotion in Mark's eyes. This is a great moment for baseball and everybody knows that. It's something I'm not going to forget."

He was gracious again in 1999 when the Cardinals and the Cubs again ended the season playing each other. Mark and Sammy each hit a homer in the final game. Mark again finished first in home runs, ending the season with 65 homers to Sammy's 63.

"I am a happy man, not disappointed," Sammy said. "I had a great year. For me, that's something to be happy about."

SAMMY CLAUS

Although 1999 was a great year, the 1998 season had been unforgettable for Sammy. He won many honors besides the MVP award. One of the most important was the Roberto Clemente Man of the Year award (*see box on page 117*). The award was given to Sammy for his charity work, including his aid to the victims of Hurricane Georges. "I'll never forget where I come from," Sammy said months later. "I'm still hungry, and I'm still humble." Sammy is such a generous man that children in his country often call him "Sammy Claus." He delivers presents to kids at Christmas and buys computers for schools.

In July 1999, Hall of Fame pitcher Juan Marichal [MAR-eh-shawl] expressed his feelings during a tribute to Sammy in New York City. His words expressed the feelings of many. "Sammy Sosa, you are a hero to everybody," Juan said, "not only because you play great baseball, but because you are a great human being."

SAMMY SLAMS

Sammy continued his greatness during the 2000 and 2001 seasons. In 2000, he batted .320 with 50 homers and 138 RBIs. Sammy won his first home run title, leading both leagues. In June, he knocked in the 1,000th–RBI of his major league career — on the 11th anniversary of his first major league game!

But with all of his success, Sammy was unhappy — and angry — about the way some things were going. Many people criticized Sammy, saying that he was concerned only about hitting home runs, or that he struck out too much, or that he wasn't a very good fielder. A lot of tension between Sammy and the Cubs developed when they did not quickly offer him a new contract for the kind of money that Sammy felt he deserved. In June, the Cubs started talking to the New York Yankees about trading Sammy to the Yanks. Sammy was confused and hurt. He wanted to stay in Chicago, but the Cubs seemed to be ignoring him.

"My question was, 'Why?' I've been working so hard. Why can't [the Cubs] come to me [with an offer]?" Sammy said.

The trade talks between the Cubs and Yankees ended in late June, but that only left Sammy uncertain about his future in Chicago. Did the Cubs want him? That's when the 2000 All–Star Game became a turning point in Sammy's career. Sammy put on an awesome display of power,

A MONTH FOR THE RECORD BOOKS

Do you think Slammin' Sammy had a great month in June 1998? No, it was an unbelievable month! He homered in his first and last at-bats and smacked 20 homers, a big-league record for the most homers in one month. But Sammy did more. He drove in 40 runs. He hit 21 homers over the 30-day period from May 25 to June 23. That's the most in any 30-day period in major league history. According to the Elias Sports Bureau, baseball's official keeper of statistics, the previous record had been 20 home runs in 30 days. That mark was set first by Pittsburgh's Ralph Kiner, in 1947, and then matched by Roger Maris, in 1961.

winning the All-Star Game Home Run Derby, by beating Ken Griffey, Jr. in the finals. "After I won the Home Run Derby, it released me," Sammy said.

Sammy's performance at the All-Star Game and his great second half convinced the Cubs to finally come through with the kind of reward for which Sammy had worked so hard. Just before the start of the 2001 season,

Chicago signed Sammy to a $72 million four-year contract extension. For Sammy, who had come from such humble beginnings, the money meant respect and security.

"To see what this man has accomplished . . . is really remarkable," said Cubs' president Andy MacPhail. "We're talking Babe Ruth. There are precious few guys in the game who have accomplished what Sammy has . . ." Sammy had finally gotten the respect that he deserved.

Sammy showed his gratitude to the Cubs by turning in another brilliant season in 2001. He hit .328, crushed 64 homers, and drove in 160 runs. Sammy became the first player in major league history to have three 60-home run seasons. His power surge was shown in part by his three three-homer games and six two-homer games. During the season, Sammy also hit his 400th career home run and scored his 1,000 career run. He played with high energy, hustling for extra bases and making spectacular diving catches in the outfield.

In the seasons of 1999, 2000, and 2001, Sammy had put together one of the greatest three-year stretches in major league history. During those years, Sammy hit 179 homers, batted .305, scored 354 runs and knocked in 437 runs. He was in a league by himself.

Sammy has come a long way from his days in the Dominican Republic. His talent, dedication, and integrity have made him a star among stars.

"I'm so happy now . . . so proud," Sammy said in 2001. "I'm more satisfied as a person . . It doesn't get any better than that."

>> GLOSSARY

astronomical unbelievably large

concussion an injury to the brain resulting from a sudden or sharp blow to the head

contagious tending to spread from person to person

gratitude thankfulness

negotiate to discuss a subject with another person in order to come to an agreement

personnel the group of people active in a business, organization, or service

rehabilitation the return to good health

vanguard the front or leading position

RESOURCES

Books

Christopher, Matt. *On the Court with Kobe Bryant*. New York, NY: Little Brown & Company, 2001.

Christopher, Matt. *On the Field with Alex Rodriguez*. New York, NY: Little Brown & Company, 2002.

Flynn, Gabriel. *Sammy Sosa*. Chanhassen: MN: Childs World, 2000.

Kernan, Kevin. *Tim Duncan: Slam Duncan*. Champaign, IL: Sports Publishing, 2000.

Rains, Rob. *Marshall Faulk: Rushing to Glory*. Champaign, IL: Sports Publishing, 1999.

Rekela, George. *Brett Favre: Star Quarterback*. Berkeley Heights, NJ: Enslow Publishers, 2000.

>> RESOURCES

Savage, Jeff. *Sports Great Ken Griffey, Jr.* Berkeley Heights, NJ: Enslow Publishers, 2000.

Schnakenberg, Robert. *Mia Hamm.* Broomall, PA: Chelsea House, 2000.

Magazine

Sports Illustrated for Kids
135 West 50th Street
New York, NY 10020
(800) 992–0196
http://www.sikids.com

>> RESOURCES

Web Sites

Sports Illustrated for Kids
http://www.sikids.com
Check out the latest news, cool games, and much more.

Take a look at the official Web sites of the following organizations:

Major League Baseball
http://www.mlb.com

National Basketball Association
http://www.nba.com

National Football League
http://www.nfl.com

Women's United Soccer Association
http://www.wusa.com